flaminio gundy

Pula

With Fazana and Bale

PULA
With Fazana and Bale

by Flaminio Gundy

Kindle Direct Publishing, USA, 2019

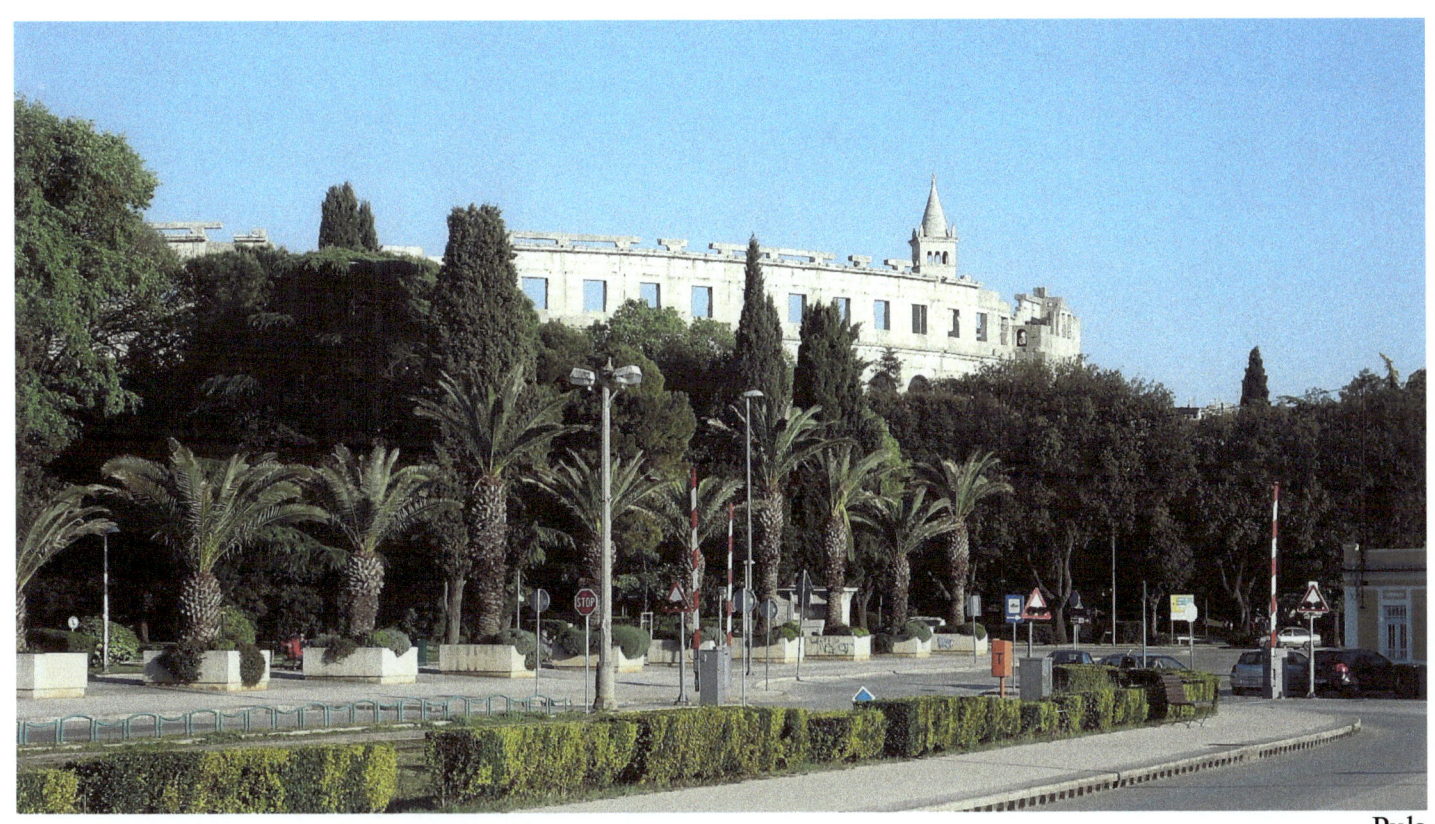

Pula

Even in Istria many dishes accompany the religious festivities, such as cod served on Christmas Eve and Good Friday and the pork on New Year, while donuts are mainly prepared during carnival festivities.

Raw ham and eggs are used for Easter with the dessert called *pinca*. The turkey and other poultry are served on the Christmas day with the *sarma*. Many Istrians cannot imagine any festive celebration without lamb in the oven, grilled fish, baked squid and barbeque (skewers, *cevapcici*, pork chops).

The distinguishing principles of Istrian cuisine would in general be the prevalence of boiled foods on ones roasts, many spices, wild herbs, enough fish, strictly wine vinegar and olive oil.

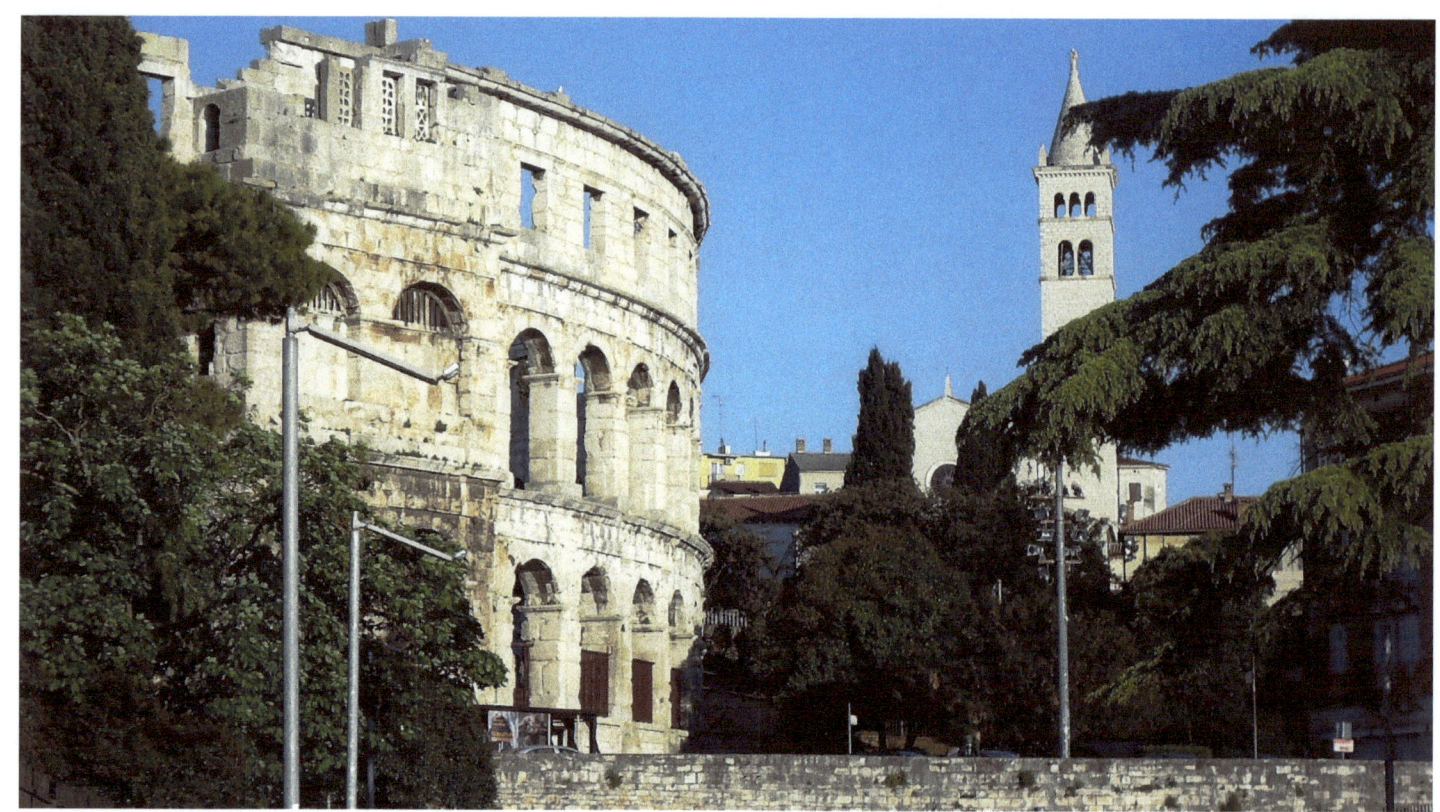

Pula

In Istria there is the possibility to enjoy the fresh and delicious seafood prepared in *buzara* style, which is not a dish, but simply a way of preparing seafood, usually prawns and shells, with white wine, garlic, olive oil and parsley.

Excellent wines, such as white malvasia, by straw yellow color, the pleasant aroma to acacia flower. Another typical wine of Istria is *teran*, a wine of an intense color ranging from purple to ruby red, of a lively fruit aroma. Also worth mentioning is the red burgundy, the red hrvatica and other less known vines. In the Istrian peninsula, many world-class high quality grapes are cultivated, such as white pinot, chardonnay, pinot gray and merlot, refosco and cabernet sauvignon.

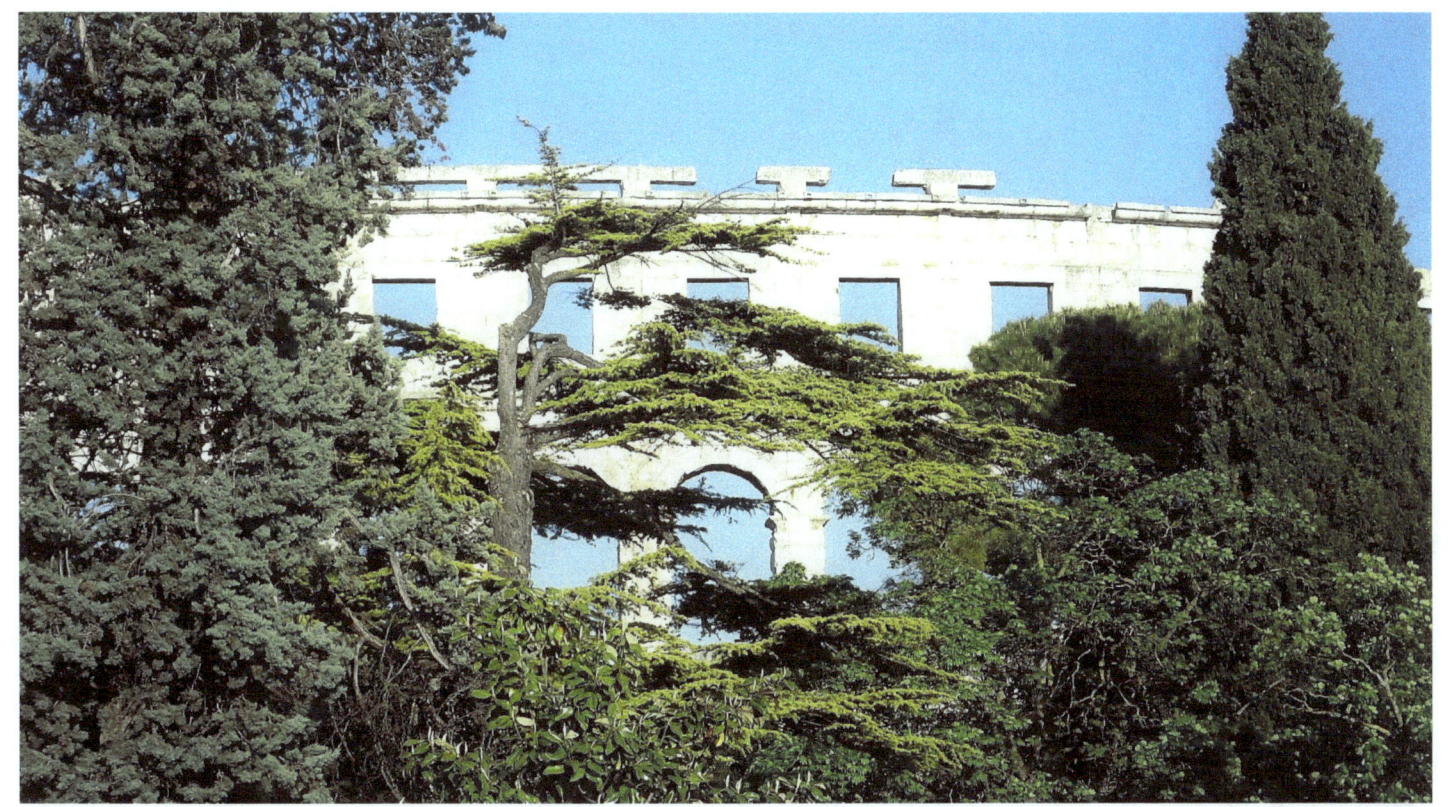

Pula

Two vines of muscat by the surprising aroma, that is Momjan's Muscat and that pink of Poreč, capture the attention of lovers of the good glass. According to experts everything depends on the soil, whose colors vary from an intense dark red in the coastal areas to a gray white to inside. Red earth is best suited for growing black grapes, while white ground is ideal for white grapes.

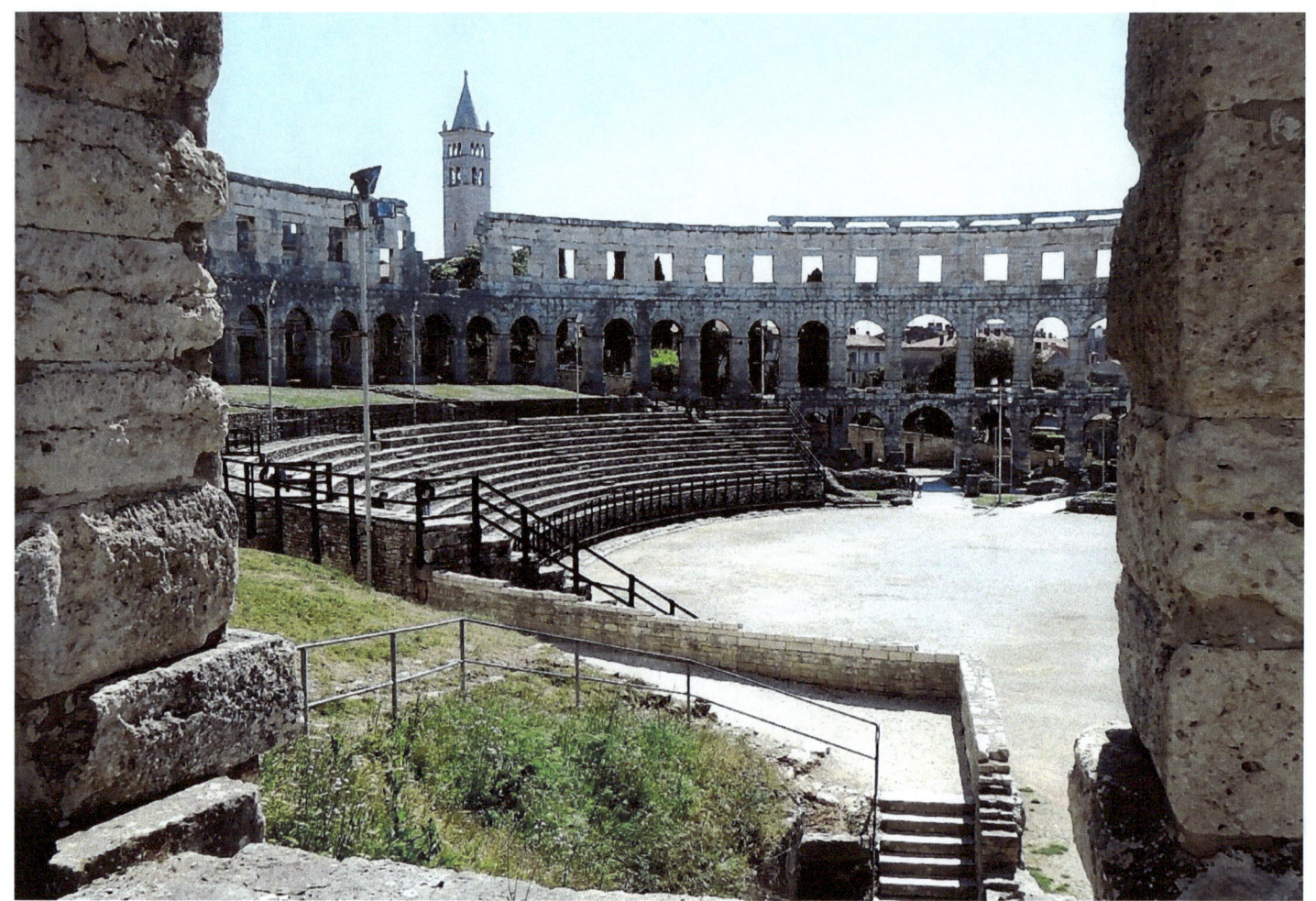

Pula

The olive oil of Istria, always symbol of this region, is considered one of the best in the world and its production began at the time of the Romans. Nothing can compete with this liquid, which is simply invincible. Its flavor is bitter and combines perfectly with many dishes. The indigenous varieties are the *Belica*, the *Karbonaca*, the *Buža* and others. Olive oil is a body care product, a remedy for many maladies and, for many, a long life elixir.

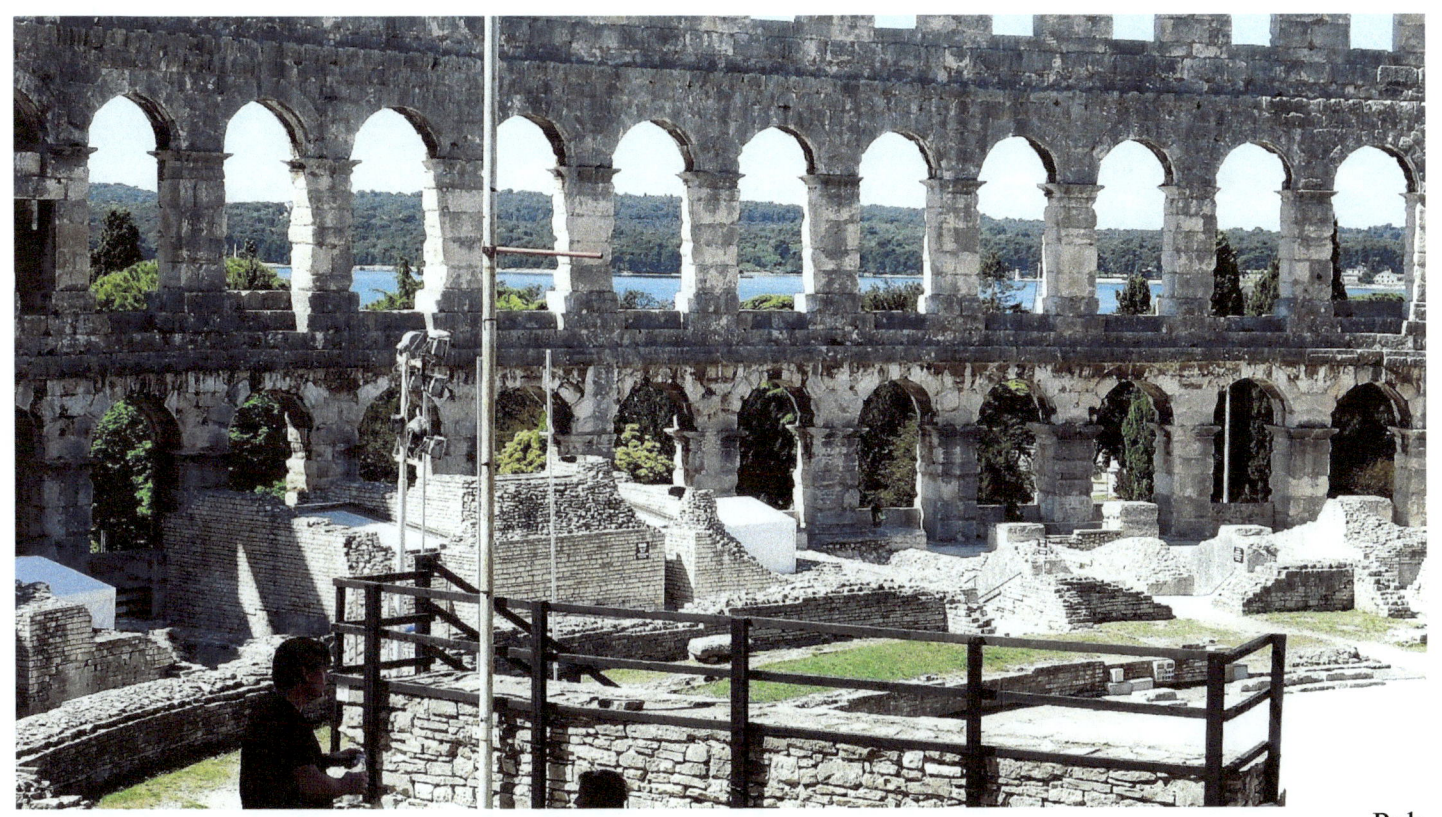

Pula

Pasta is one of the most characteristic hot dishes of Istrian cuisine. You can taste it in its many forms and with a large amount of sauces. Among the homemade pasta we find various varieties including *ravioli* with asparagus, *posutice* (square shaped pasta), *fuzi* in deer sauce or truffle, *pljukanci* in ham sauce or with asparagus.

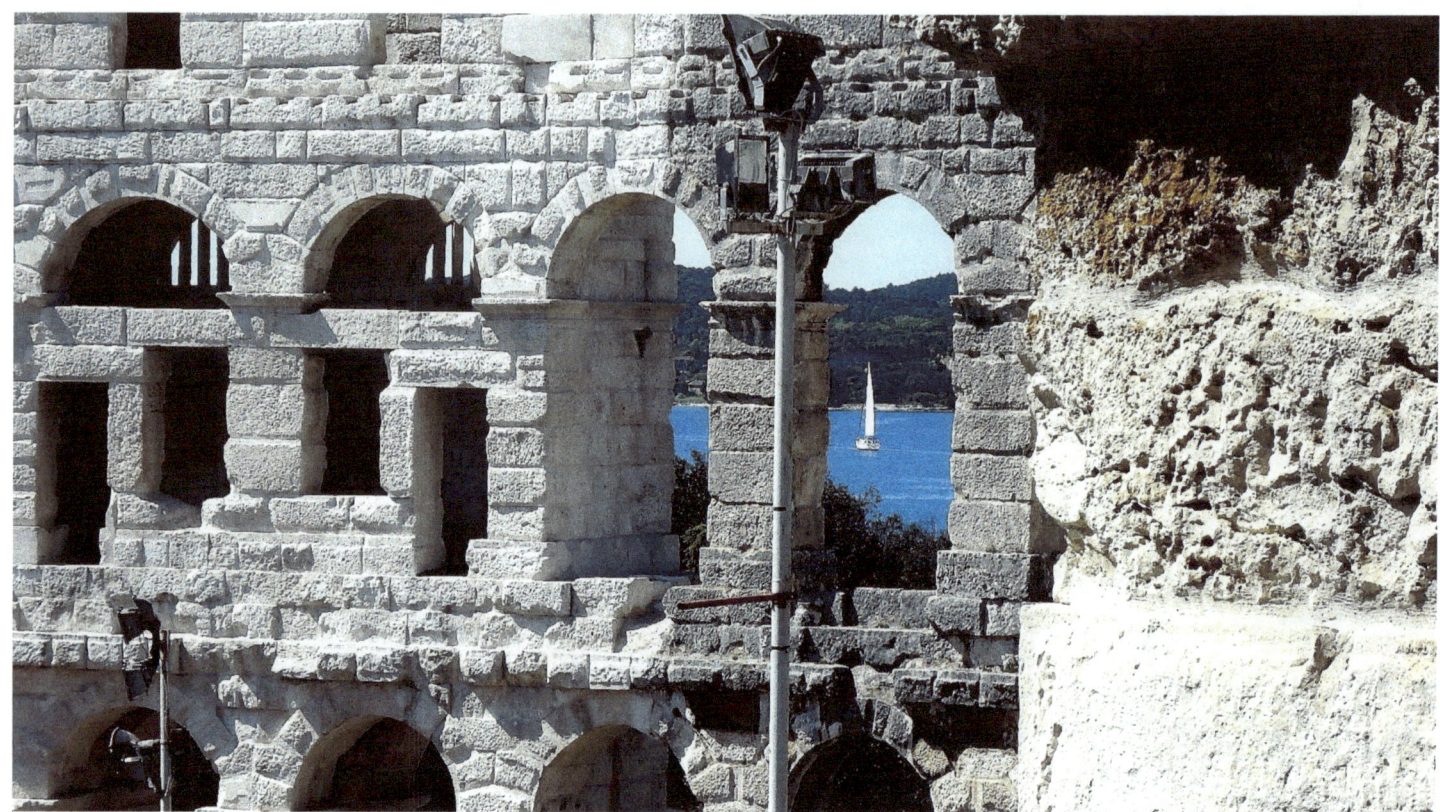

Pula

The risottos are a specialty of Istria. The famous black risotto is made with cuttlefish (similar to squid) that releases a black liquid like ink, making a tasty black velvet risotto.

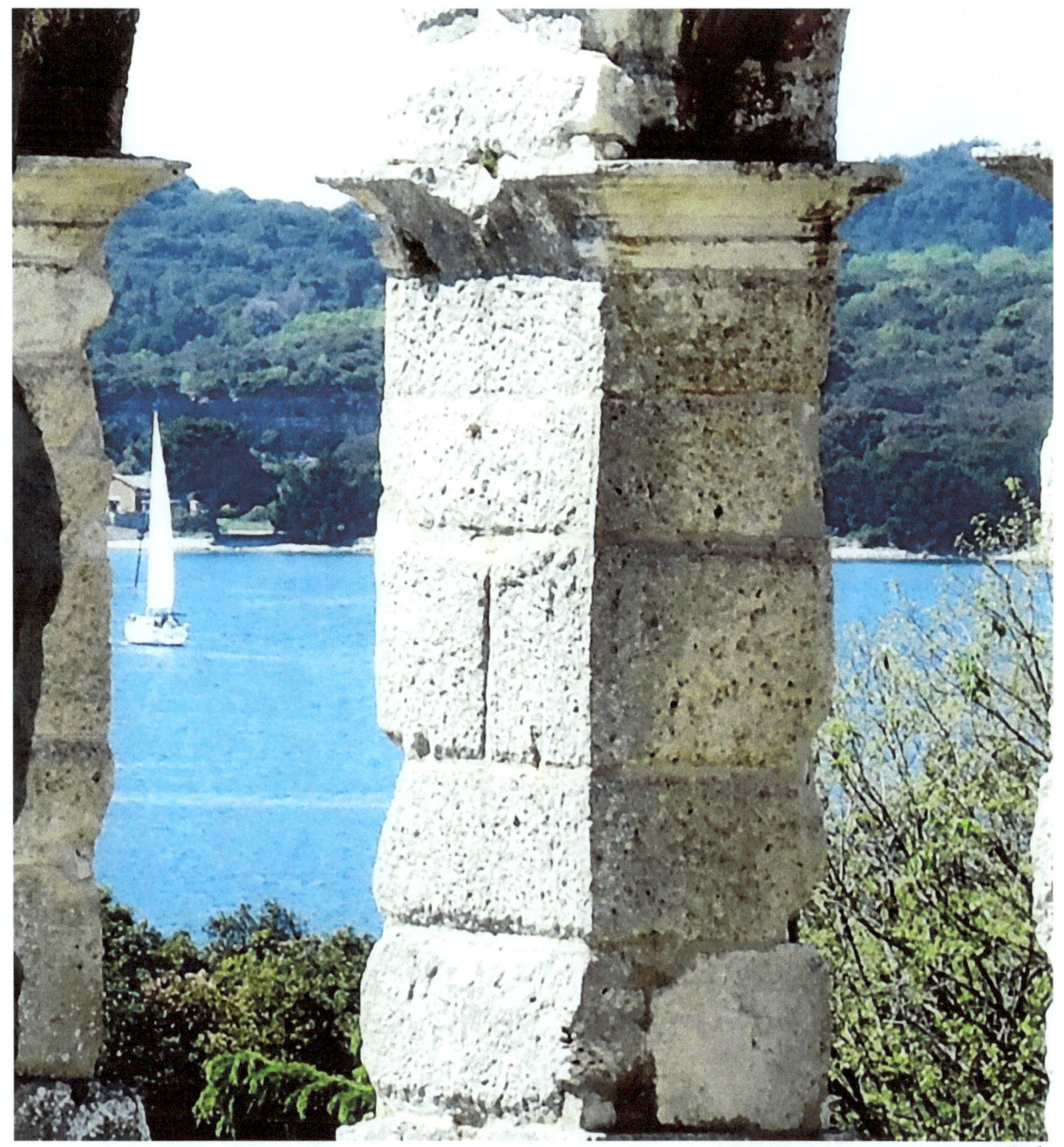

Pula

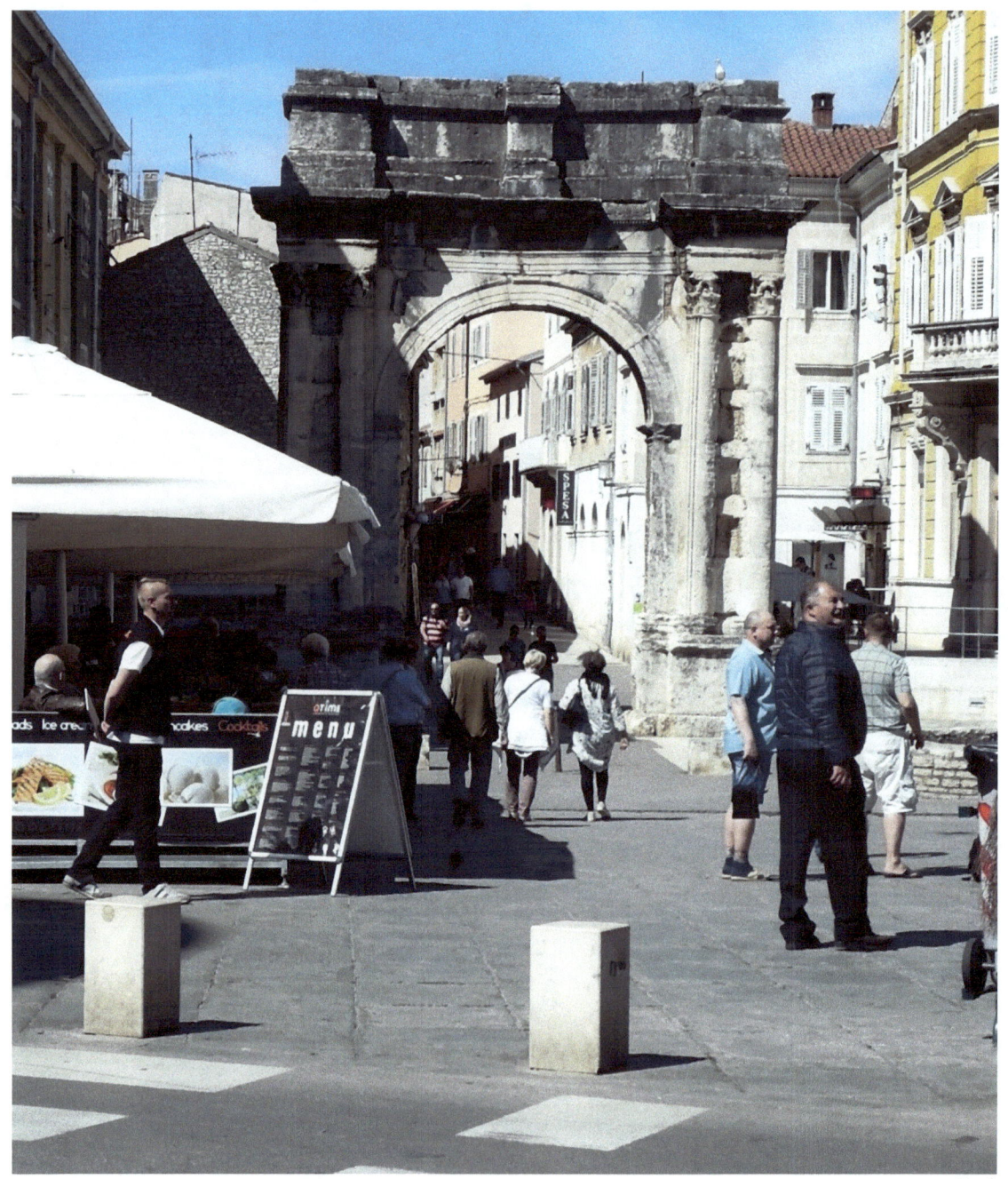

Pula

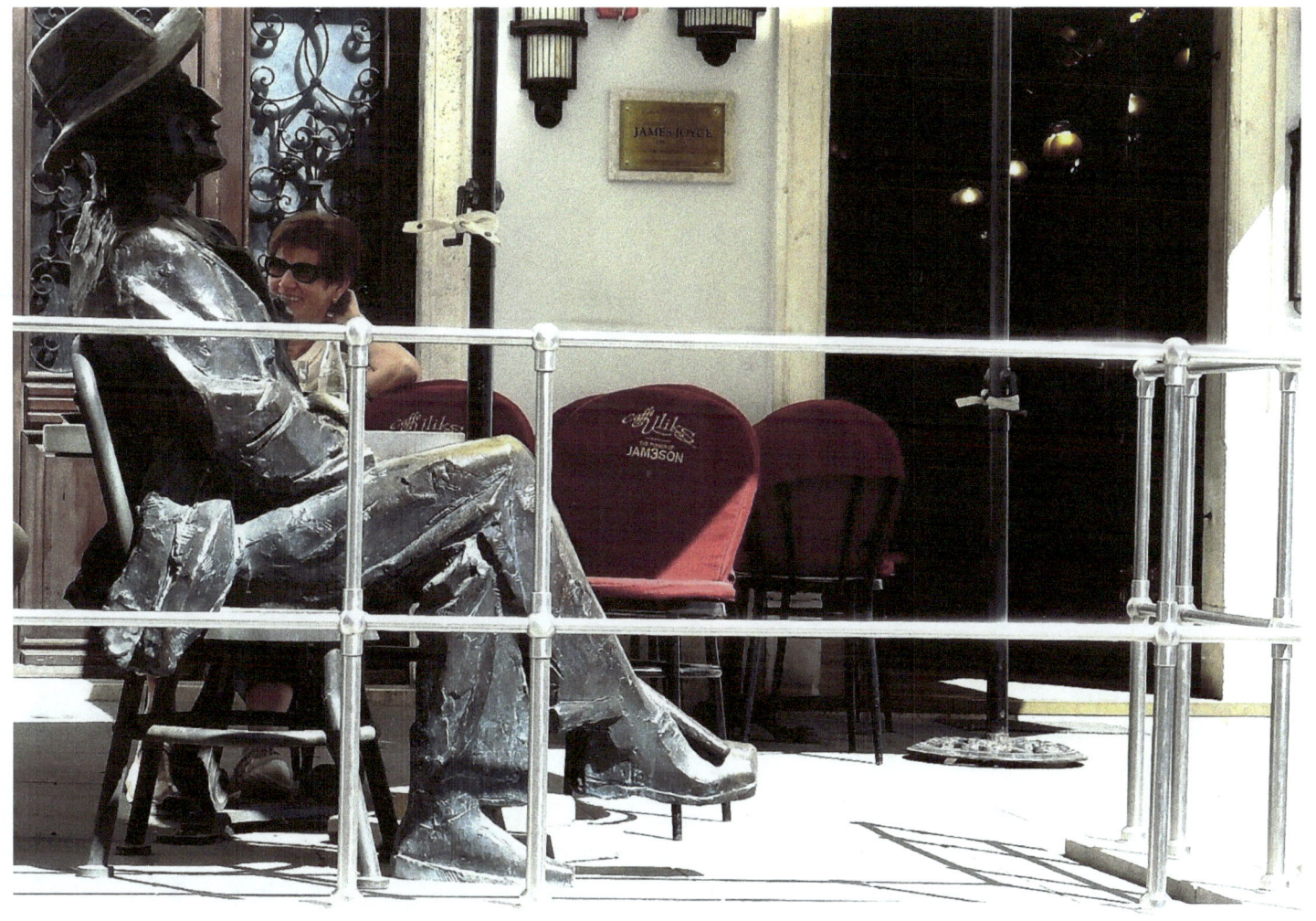

Pula

Soups are the strong dish of Istrian cuisine and are prepared with meat and vegetables. Their peculiarity lies in the fact that they are prepared with a pesto made with dry bacon to small pieces, garlic and one parsley leaf. Very tasty the *maneštra*, delicious bean soup, potatoes and seasonal vegetables, sometimes with meat. The typical Istrian soups you can order in the taverns are the young corn soup, fennel soup, chickpea soup and many other varieties. If it is prepared with acid kale, the soup is called *jota*.

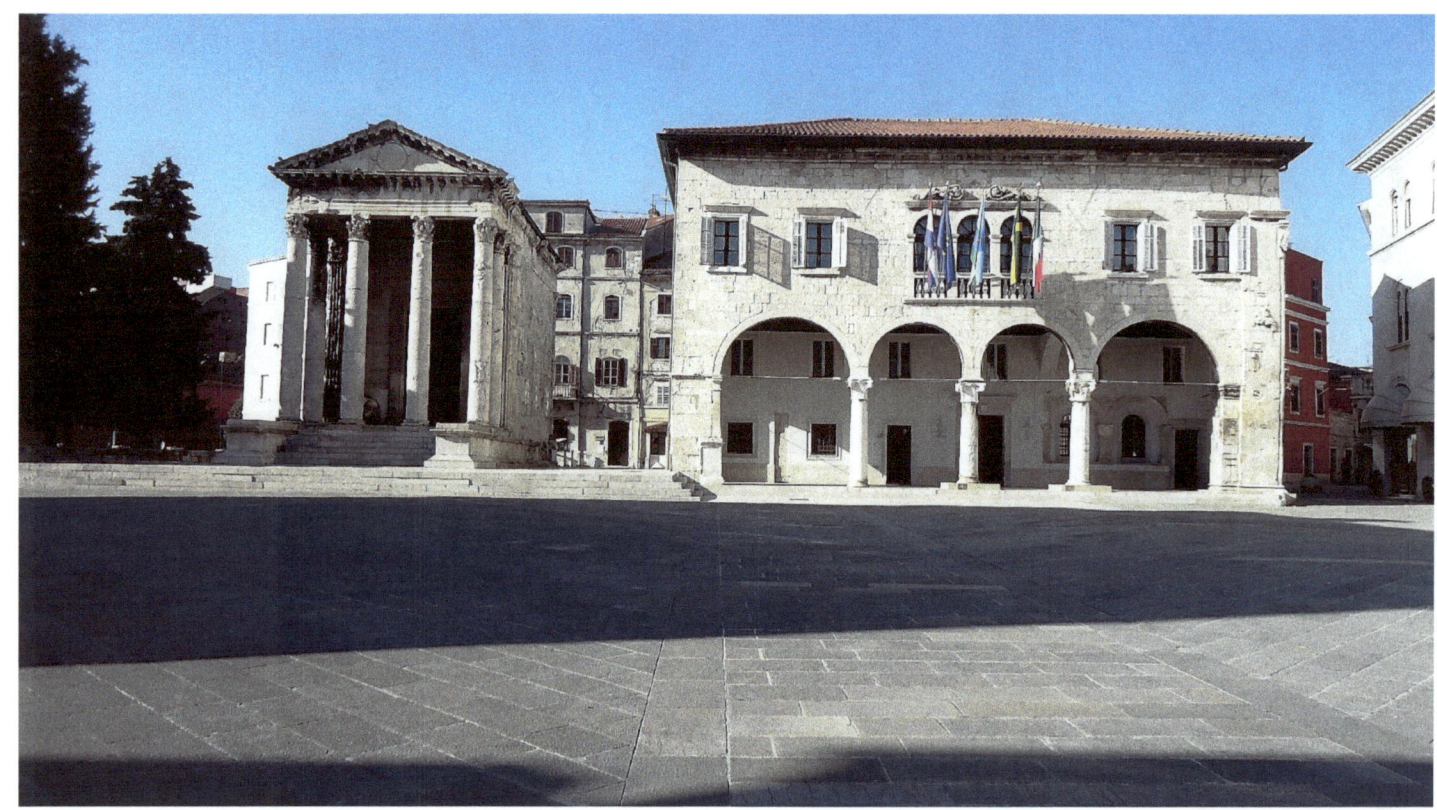

Pula

In the land of Istria is produced an excellent ham, especially in the hinterland around Dignano d'Istria, also thanks to bora that favors the drying outdoors. It is distinguished by the thin meats and seasoning with a brine enriched with pepper, rosemary, laurel and garlic. It is produced in the winter, starting from the first days of fresh bora, dried in the following 5 months and seasoned 12 months. And strictly hand-cut. It is served at thin slices with sheep cheese and olives as a cold appetizer.

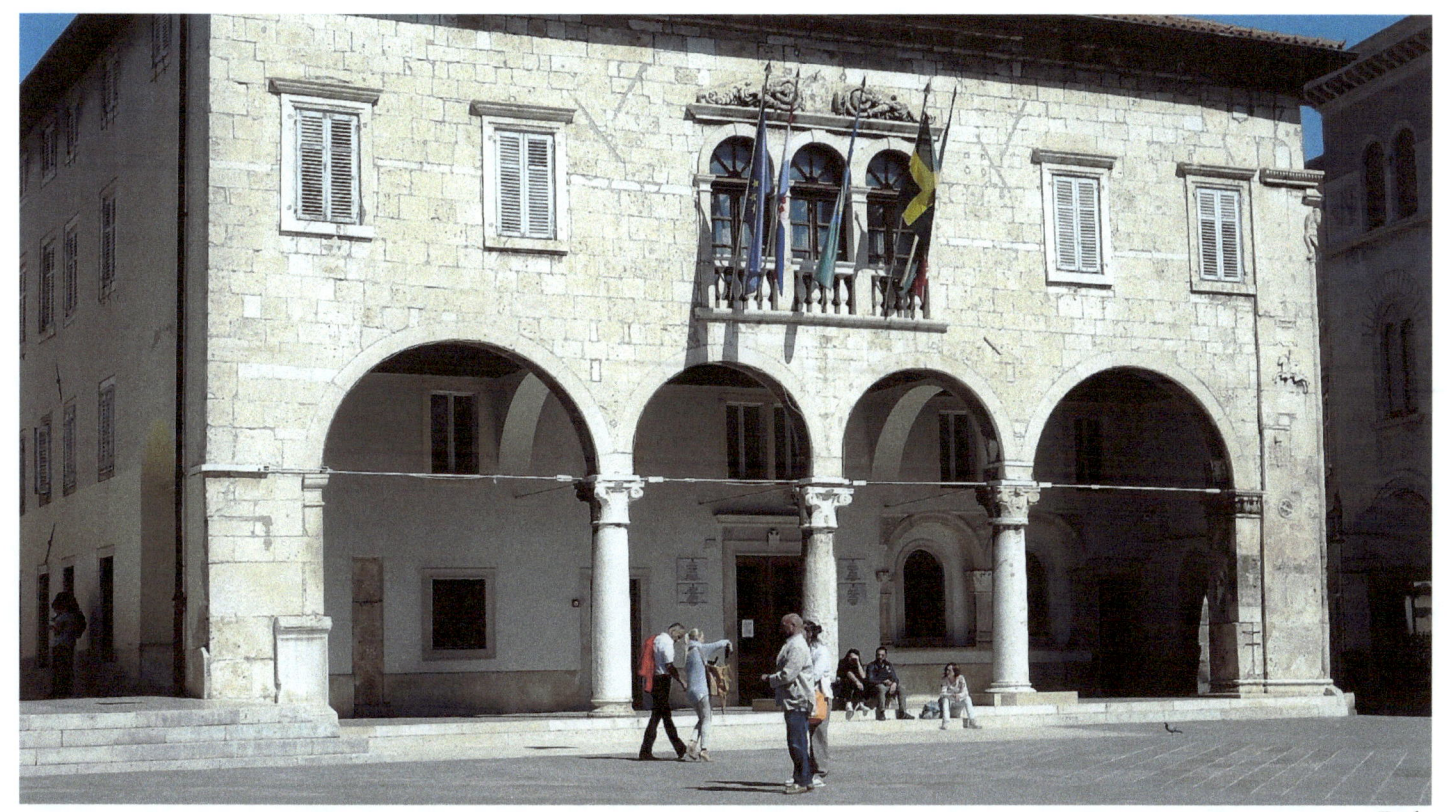

Pula

Bobiči, corn soup. In a large pot, fry lightly in olive oil the garlic and parsley, add the peeled potatoes, washed and cut into pieces, the new shelled beans, the new grains of corn, the smoked pork or ham bone, the peeled tomatoes cut into pieces or tomato sauce, salt, pepper, water and cook slowly over medium heat for 2-3 hours. When the *bobiči* are almost cooked, remove potatoes from the pot with a ladle, crush them and put them back in the pot to thicken the soup slightly.

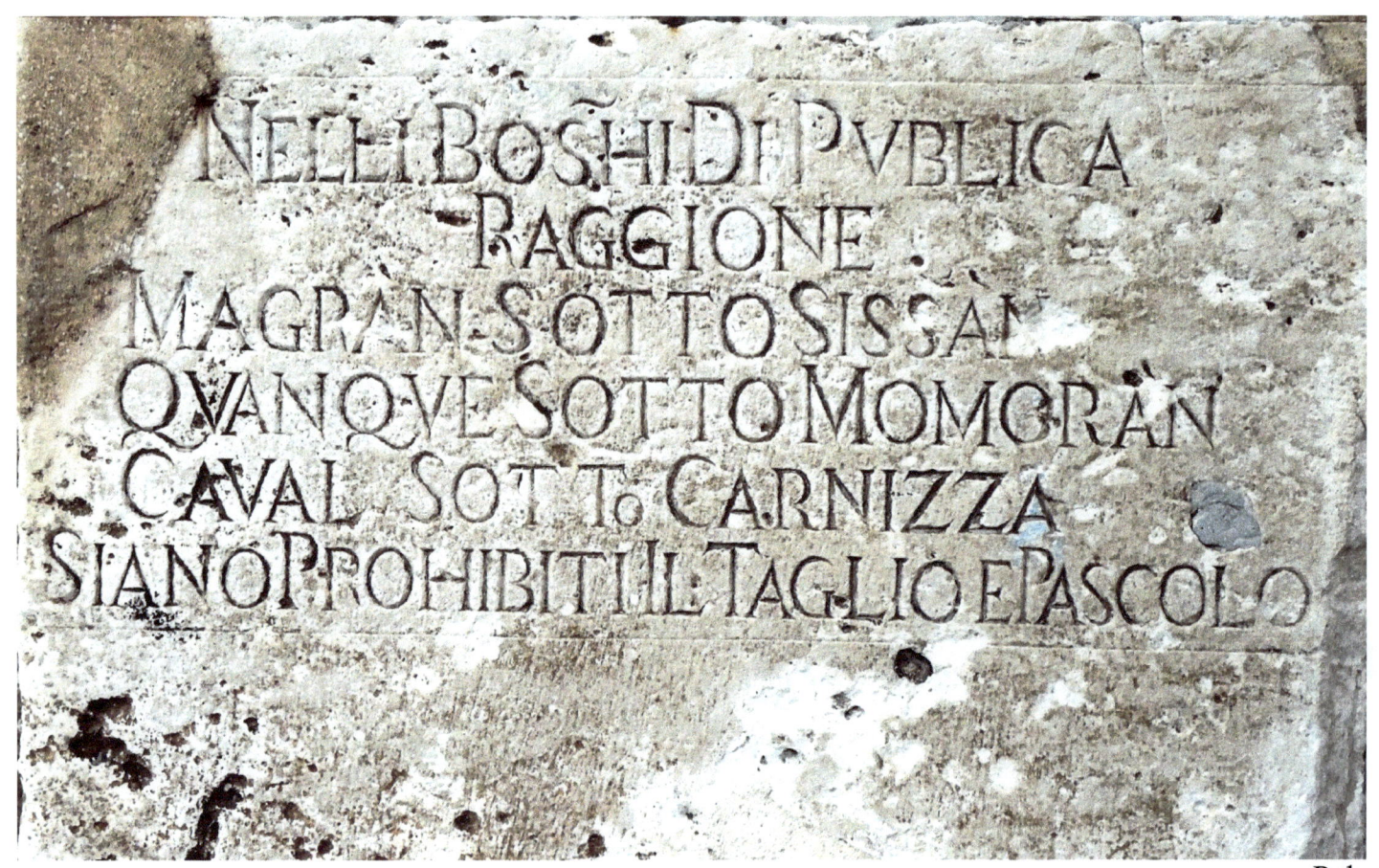

Pula

Ciabatta kruh s slani srdele i luk, ciabatta with salted sardines and onion. Prepare the flour dough with fresh yeast, a teaspoon of sugar, lukewarm water, and olive oil. Salty and let it leaven. Once doubled in volume split the dough into two equal parts. Place a half of the dough in a pan with a little olive oil and spread the salted sardines on the surface and the onion previously browned in olive oil. Add a trickle of olive oil and lay the second half of the dough. Let it rise a little more, then put the pan in the oven for 30 minutes at 180 ° C. Serve warm together with arugula salad and grated sheep cheese.

14

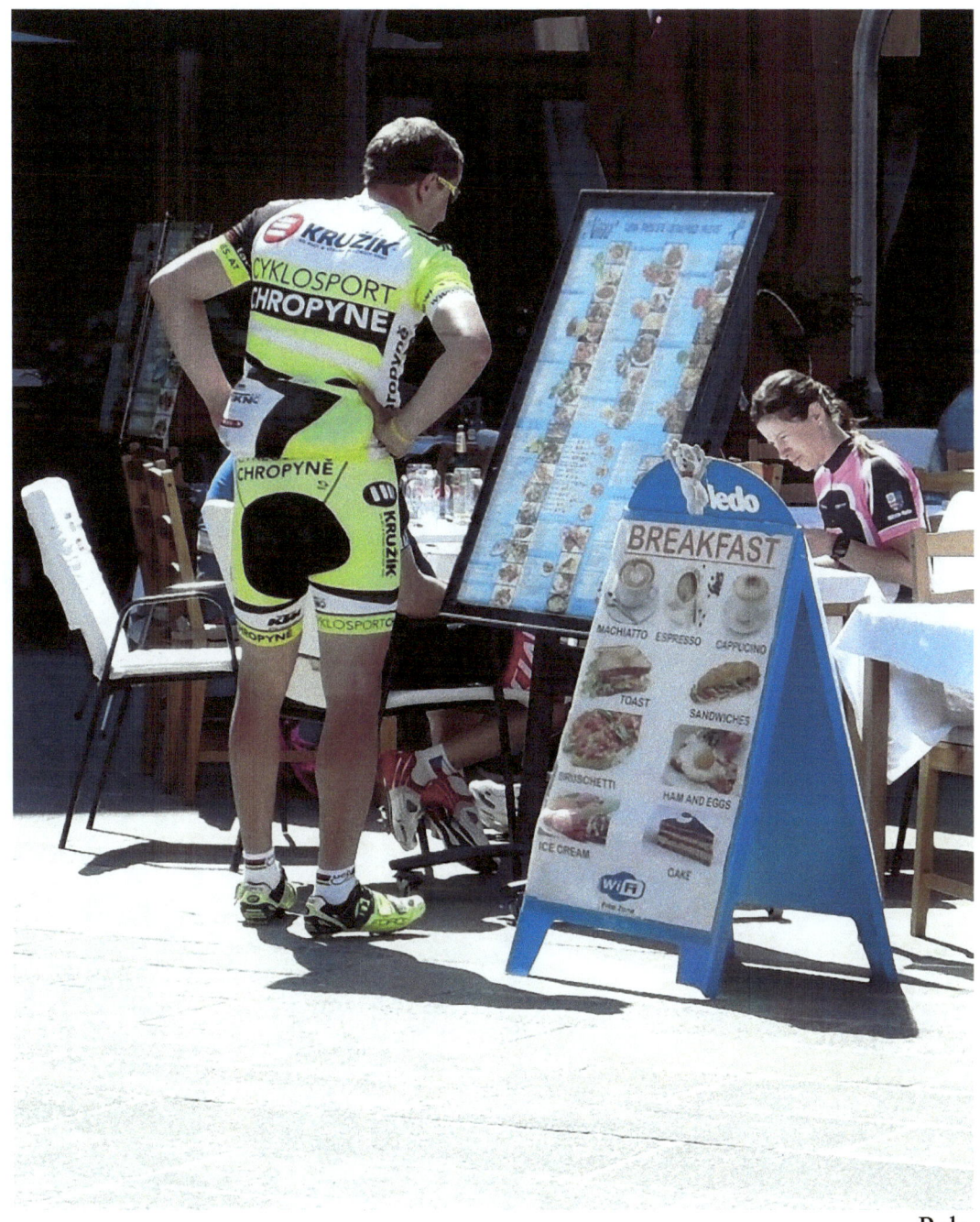

Pula

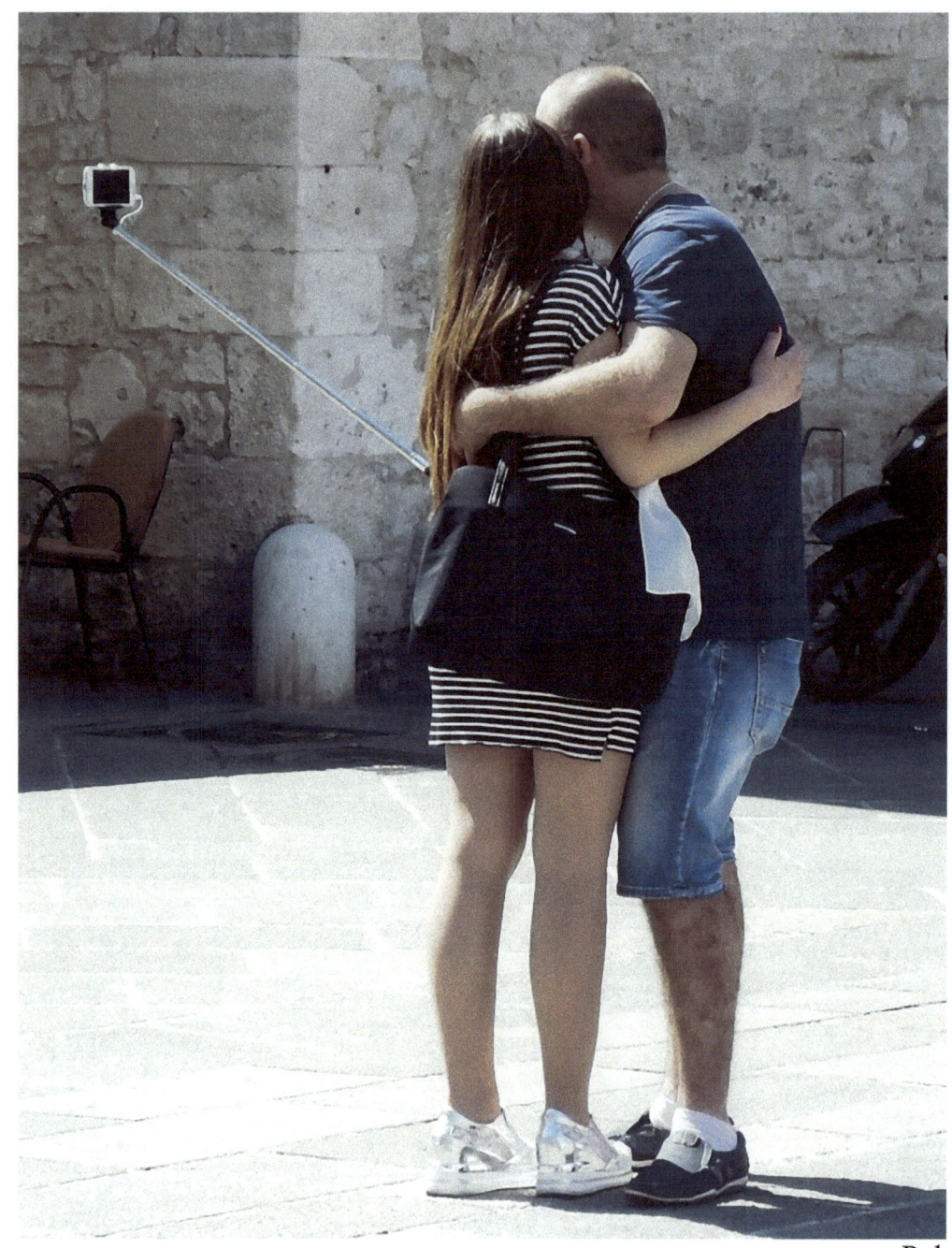

Pula

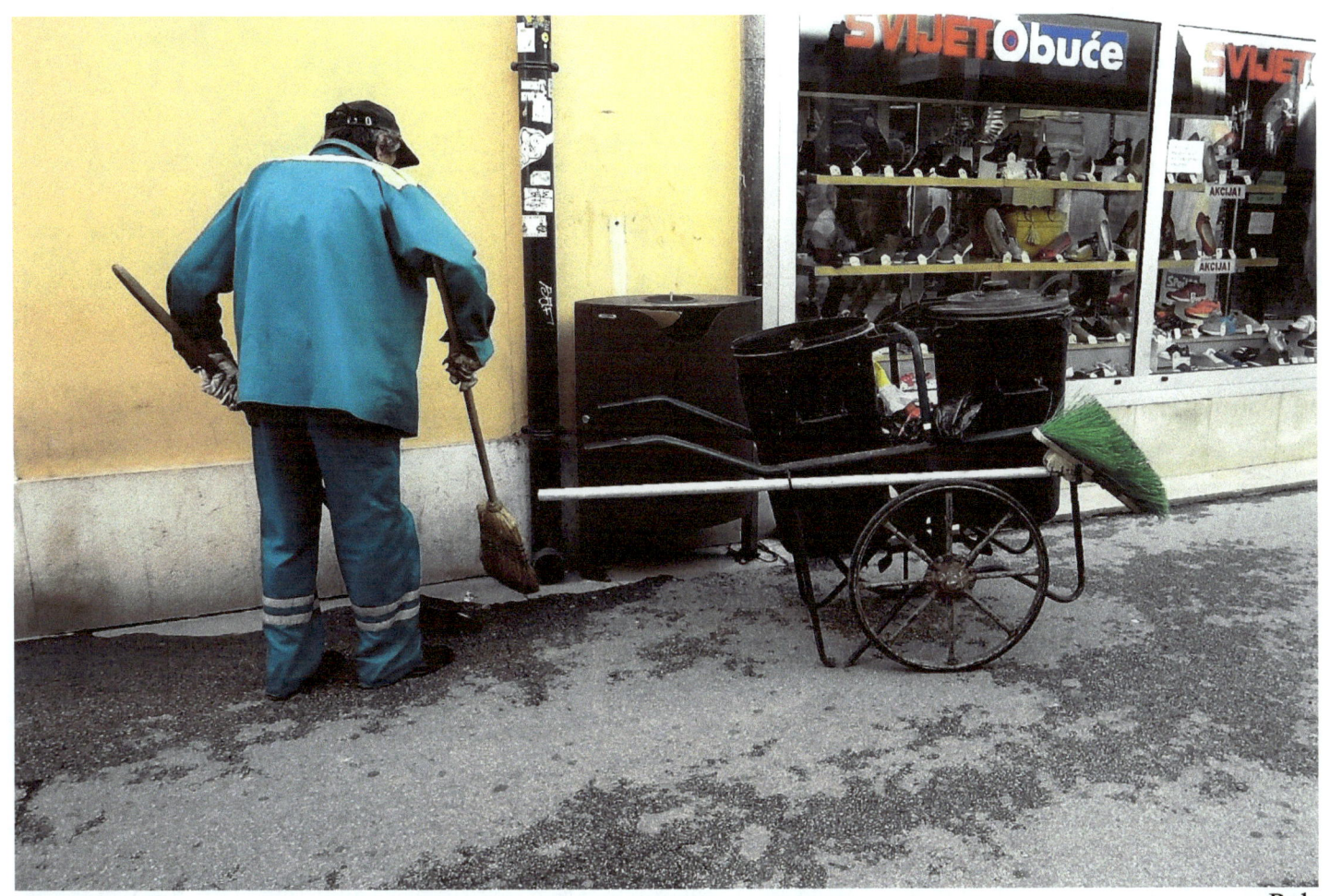

Pula

Fuži s tartufima, fresh egg pasta with truffles. Cook the *fuži* in boiling salted water with a thread of olive oil. When cooked, drain and rinse them in hot water. Add a tablespoon of olive oil and a little boiling water and stir well. Meanwhile, grate the truffles in a frying pan and after having browned them in the butter a few minutes add the cream. When the cream becomes dense (if it becomes too dense, add a few drops of white wine), salt, pepper and add a yolk of egg stirring well. Season the pasta with the obtained sauce and pour grated sheep cheese.

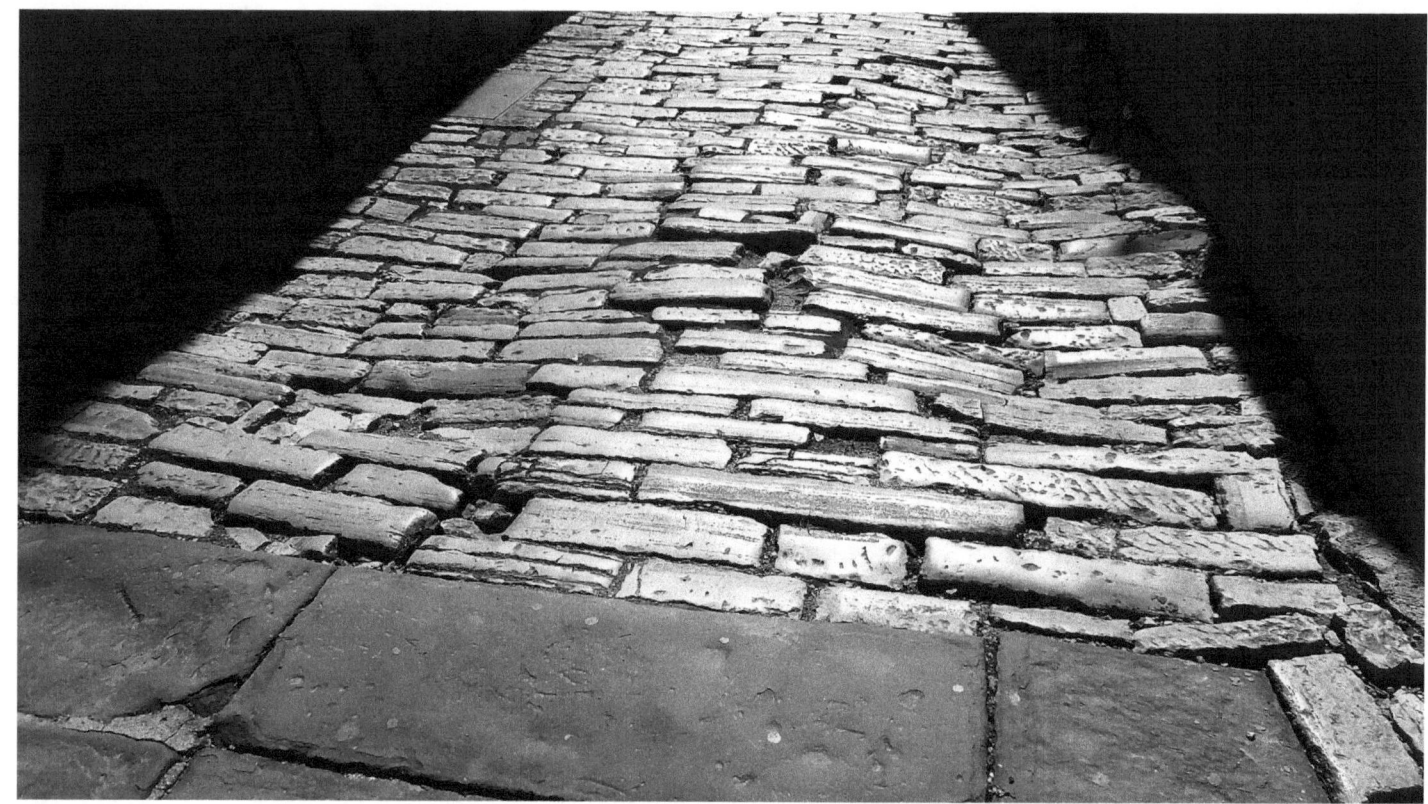

Pula

Fuži sa paprikaš kokoška, fresh egg pasta with hen stew. In a saucepan - best if by earthenware - make a sauce of oil, lard, garlic and onion. Add the chicken to pieces, a glass of dry white wine, tomato sauce, vegetable aromas and water. Let it cook in low heat for at least three hours, adjusting with the water the sauce that will result in a nearly sticky intingle, with golden brown color. Better if consumed the next day. The *fuži* should be kneaded with flour, eggs, a spoonful of oil or some wine and optional salt. Work vigorously the dough until you get a smooth compact paste that you will let rest for about an hour before rolling it up with the rolling pin. Cut it into squares or triangles that you will wrap obliquely around the handle of a wooden spoon.

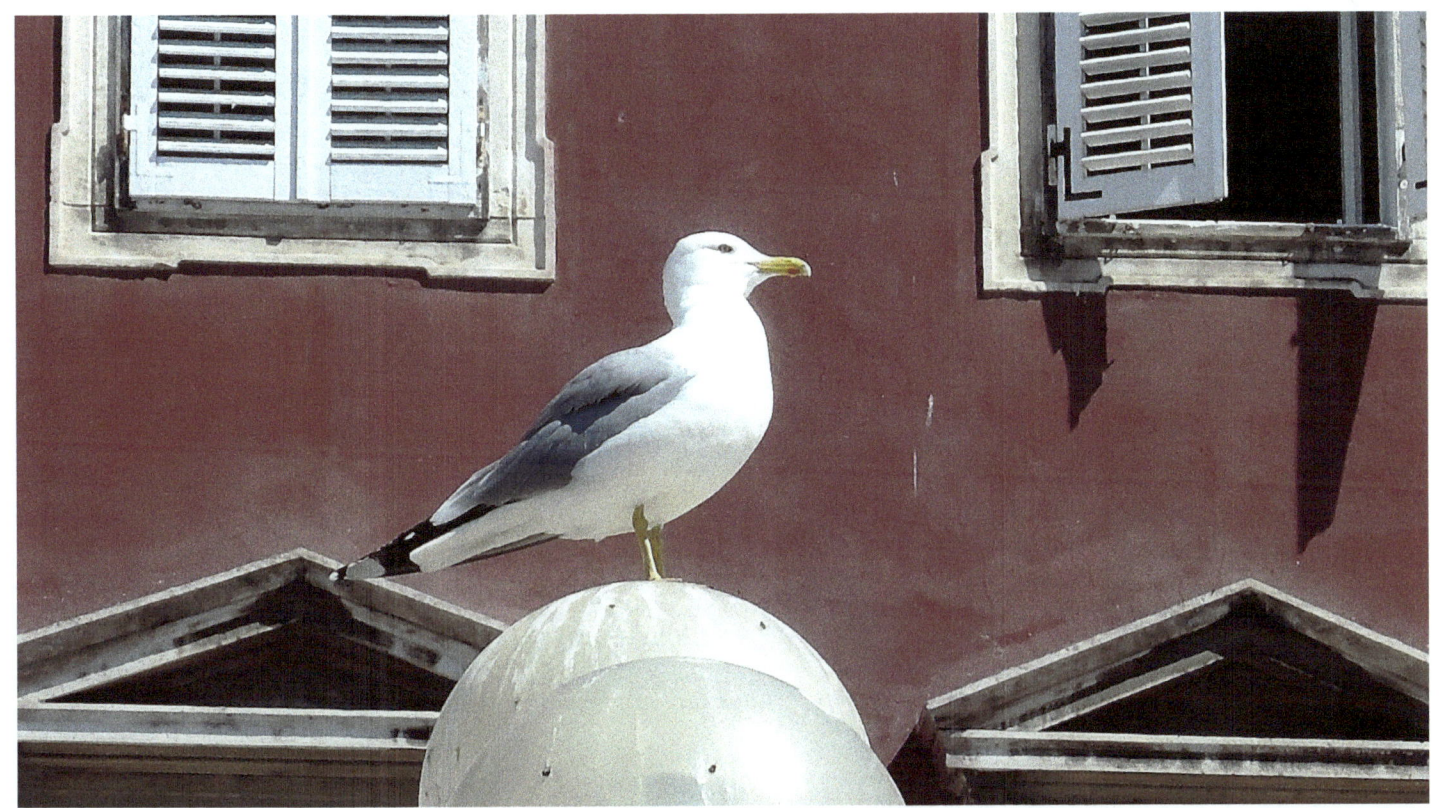

Pula

Jota, soup with beans and potatoes. Soften the dried white beans for a whole night, then drain and boil with pork rind cut into pieces. In the meantime, fry some oil in a frying pan and a spoonful of white flour, then add it to the beans with the pork. In another pan fry the lard, onion, sage, garlic and parsley and when all will be well browned add two handfuls of yellow flour. You will need add this mirepoix to beans at the end cooking. Brown the bacon in another pot, add the sour sauerkrauts, make them taste, and add it to the beans, mix and finish the cooking.

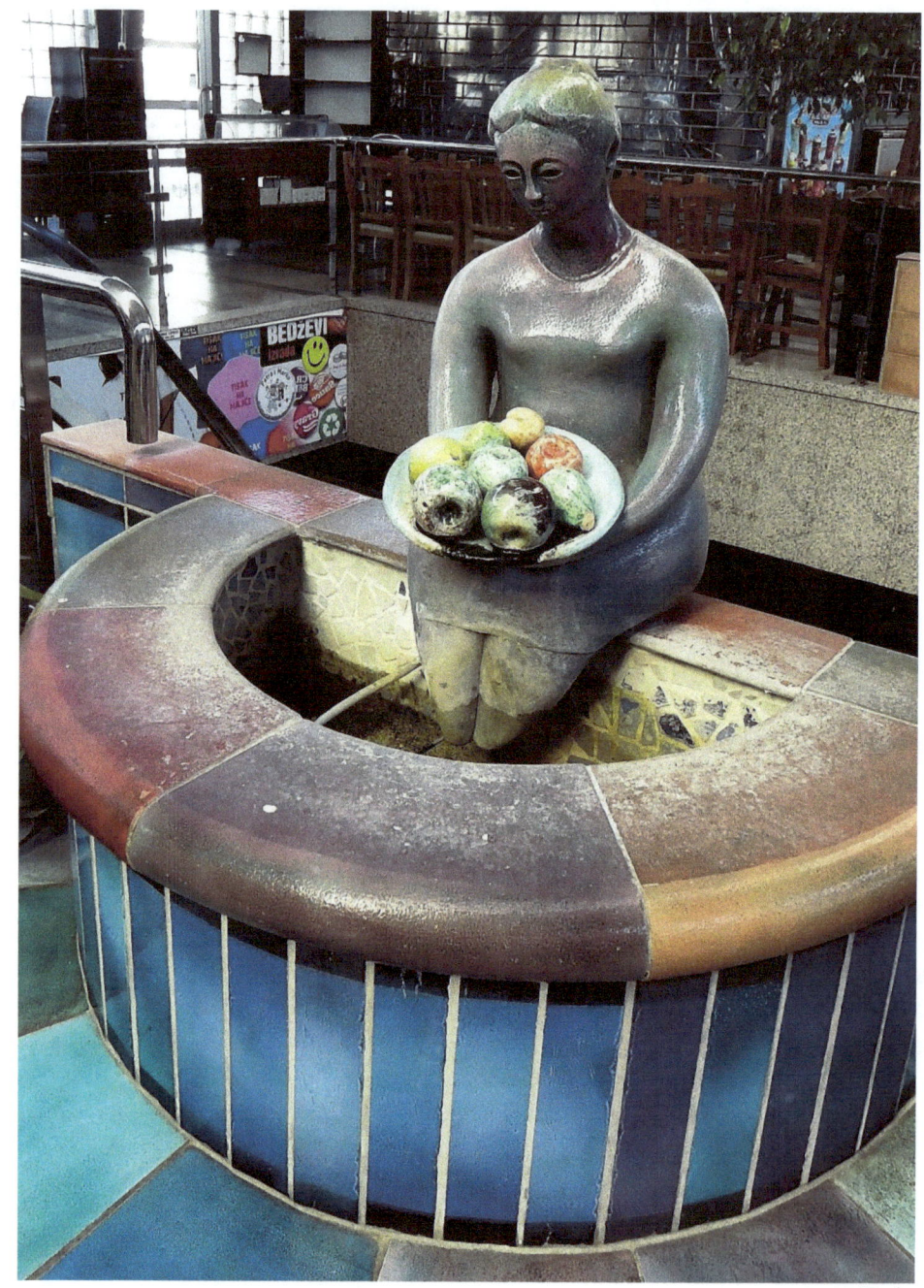

Pula

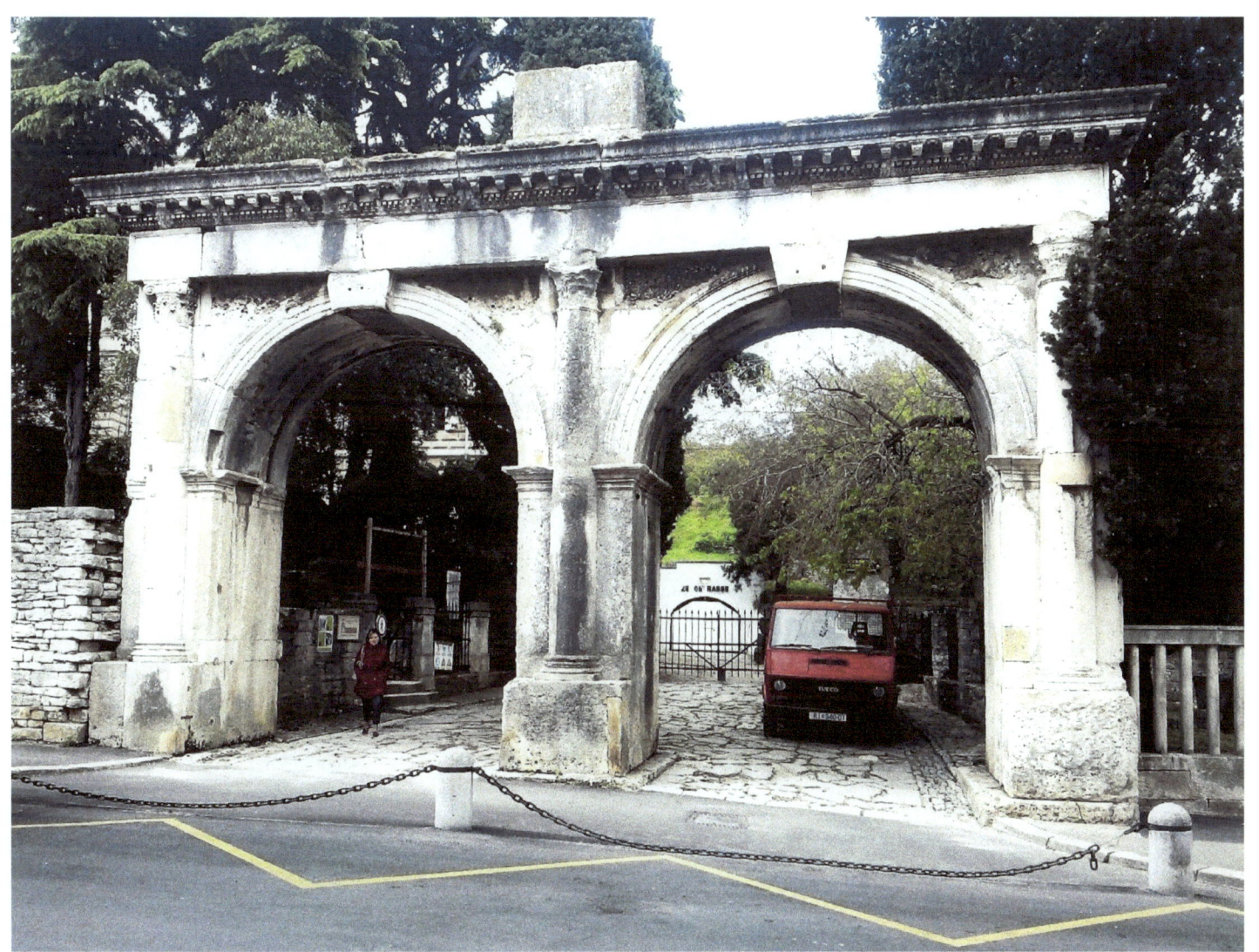

Pula

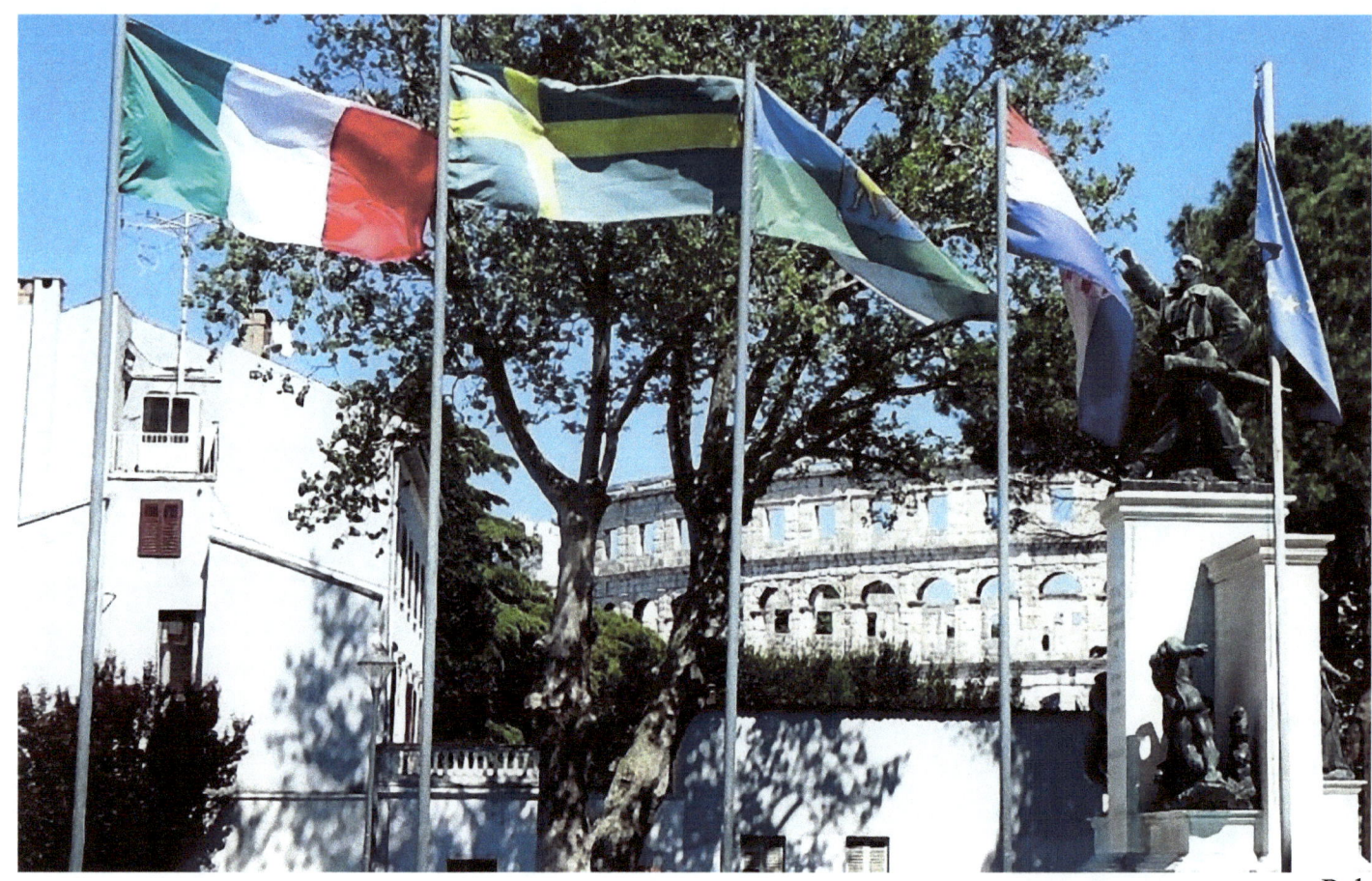

Pula

Juha od janjetine, lamb soup. Wash the lamb meat and vegetables for good and cut it into cubes. Cut the cabbage into strips. Mix egg yolks with cream and lemon juice. Chop up the parsley. Put the meat in not abundant water and bring to boiling. Remove the foam and add the vegetables at cubes, onion, garlic, bay leaf, salt, pepper and mixed spices. Boil the cabbage separately. Cook some rice in salted water, drain and rinse well under the cold running water. As soon as the meat is soften, filter the soup and place the meat and vegetables aside. Add the ready food slowly with yolk, cream and so on to the soup, stirring constantly. Then add the rice, meat, vegetables and sprinkle with chopped parsley.

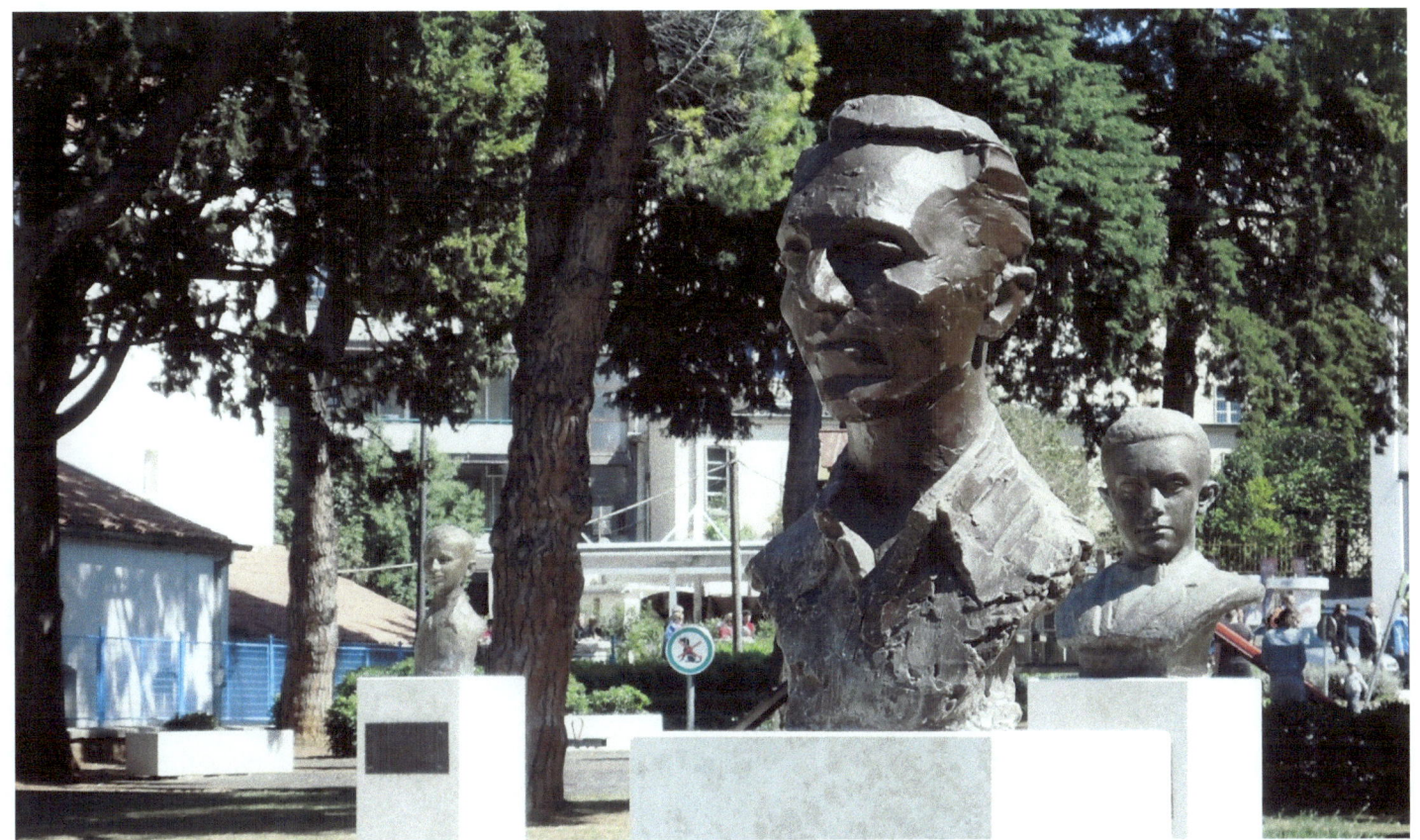

Pula

Juha od krumpira, potatoes soup. Peel and cut to dice the potatoes. Finely slice the bacon. Mince the onion, garlic and parsley. Heat the margarine and jump the bacon and onion, sprinkle with sweet red paprika and add the potatoes, mixed spices, marjoram, bay leaf, salt and pepper. Sprinkle with flour, mix well and add a good amount of water. Boil gently until the potatoes are soft. Then pour the soup into the sieve, add the cream, chopped parsley, garlic and vinegar to taste. Bring it quickly to boil and serve.

23

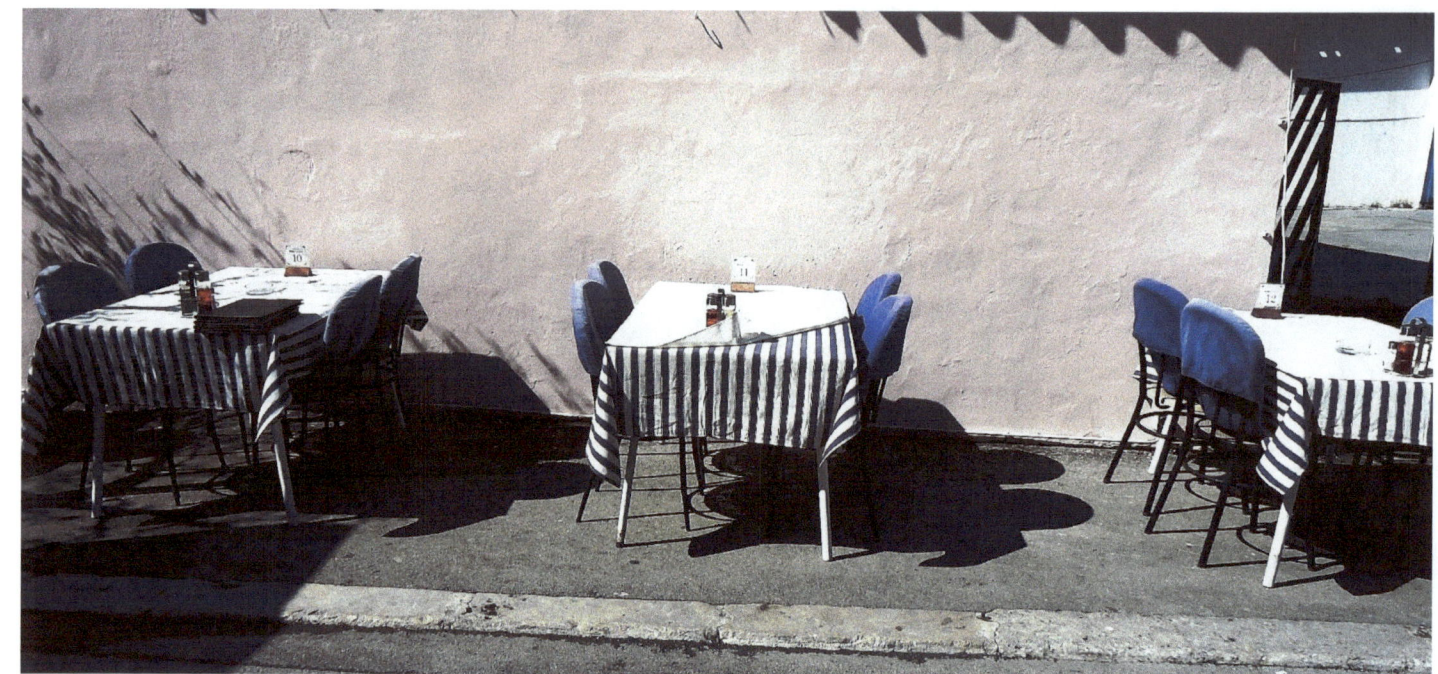

Pula

Maneštra Istarska, minestrone of beans. Soak the beans and chickpeas the previous evening for 12 hours. Prepare celery, carrot and onion for the sauce by cutting them thinly. Fry with a little oil and wither it for a few minutes. Add the diced bacon, a few tufts of rosemary and brown them. Add the legumes, season for a few minutes, then unite the lukewarm water, cover and boil at low heat for an hour and an half. About half an hour before the cooking is completed, combine the diced potatoes and adjust the salt and pepper.

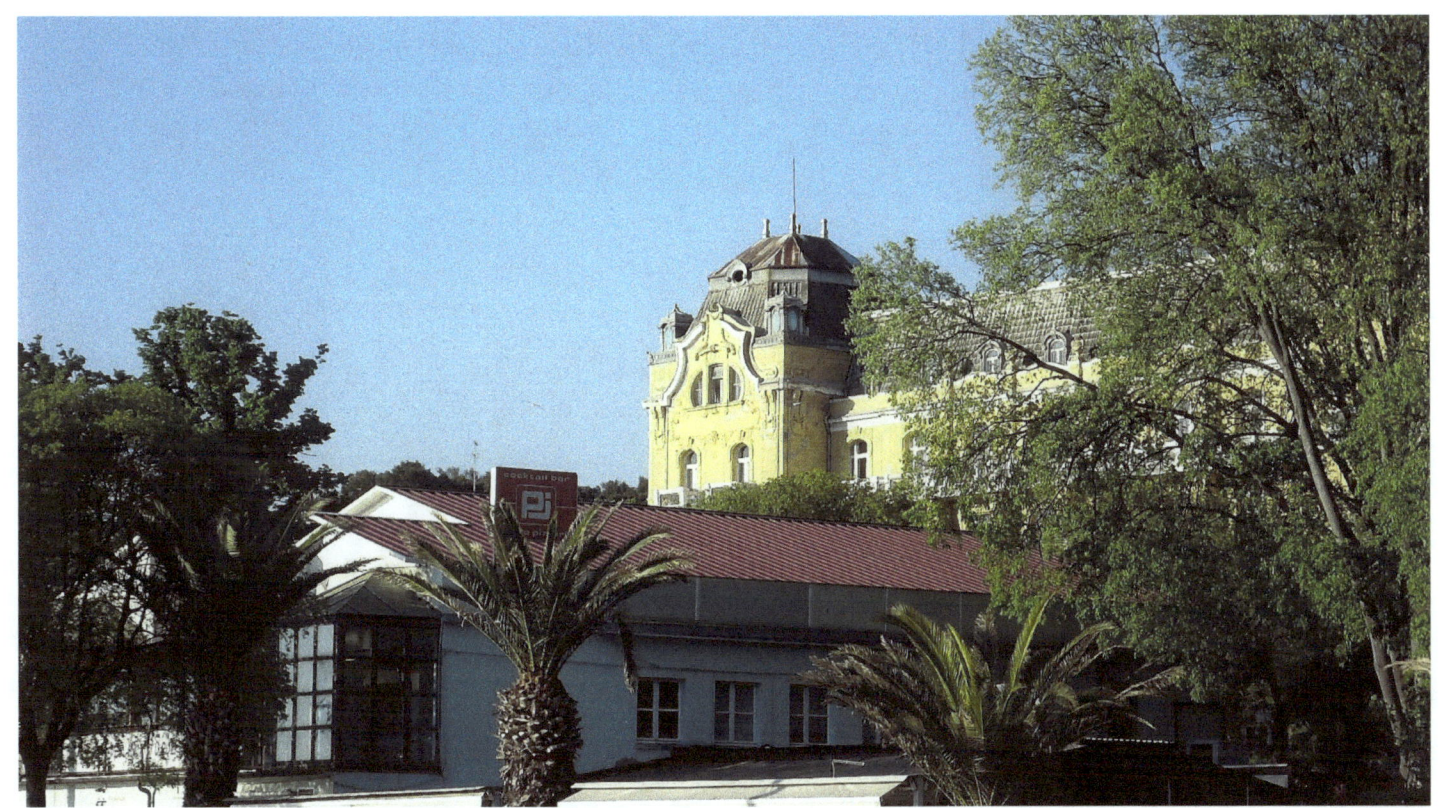

Pula

Pljukanci, Istrian homemade pasta with shrimp, clams and wild asparagus. Mix the flour with water and add an egg and a pinch of salt to taste, to form a smooth dough. Let it rest for about 15 minutes. Obtain some little balls and rub them in your hands until you get some small salamis. In a frying pan, pour a little oil and garlic, add the clean asparagus and cut into pieces and finally the tomatoes cut in half. Cook for a few minutes to mix the ingredients together. After leaving the clams in salted water for about two hours, fry them in the pan with asparagus and tomatoes, until they will be opened and shade them with white wine. Add the peeled and shredded shrimp and cook for about 15 minutes. In another pan, brown a clove of garlic and combine the shells and shrimp heads, then add warm water to make the dish more tasty. Cook the *pljukanci* in boiling water for about 7 minutes. As soon as they are ready, fry them with the sauce of clams and asparagus and serve the dish with a sprinkling of condiment of shrimp.

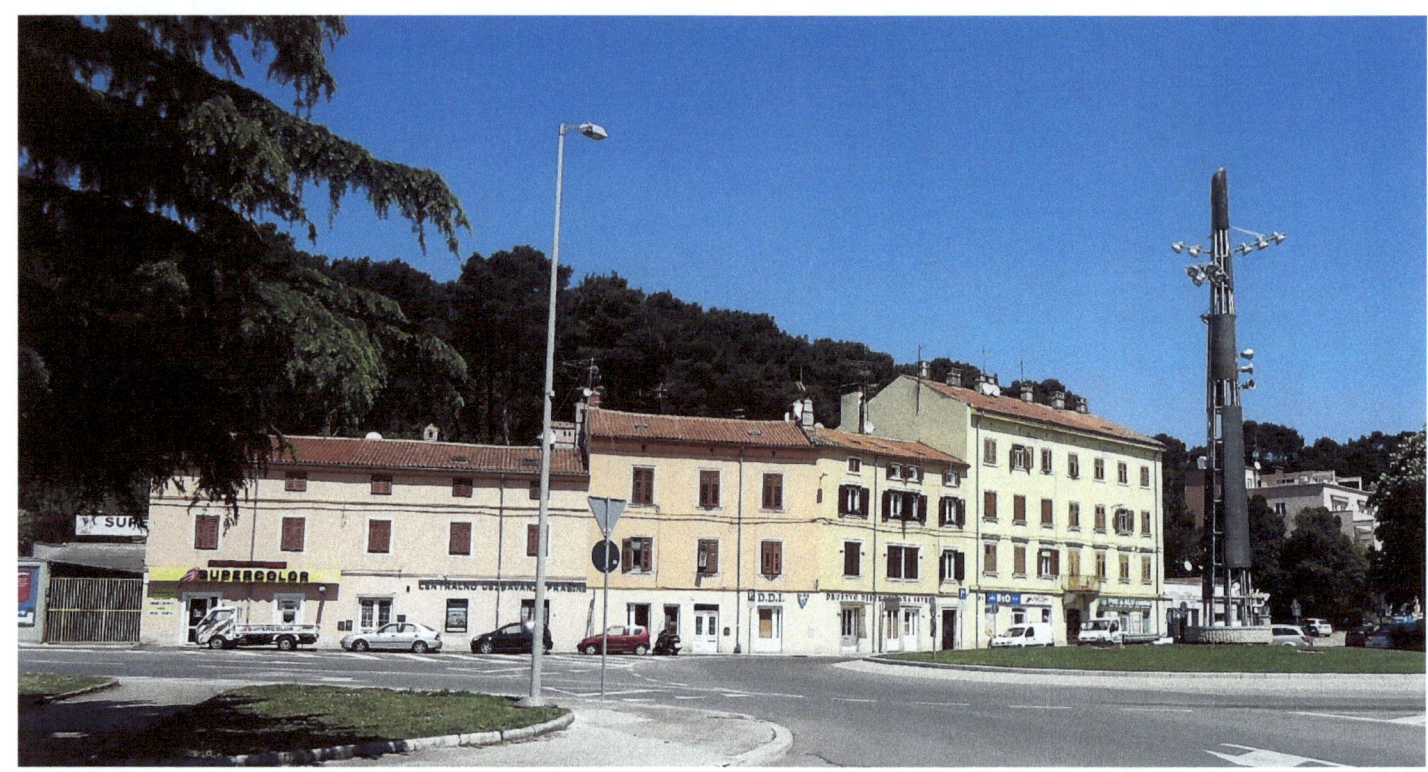

Pula

Strukli, stuffed ravioli. Sift the flour, place it like fountain on the pastry board, break an egg and amalgamate with warm water until you get a solid dough but not too hard. Cover the dough with a cloth for about half an hour, then stretch it with the rolling pin until a thin sheet is got. Using a toothed wheel, cut the puff pastry into two pieces and place them on a previously floured cloth. To prepare the filling, work the cottage cheese with egg yolks, grated Parmesan cheese and salt. Then beat the egg whites until stiff and add them gently. At this point put the filling on the two sheets of pasta and roll it up helping with the cloth as two sausages that will be "strangled" at the ends. Cut with a knife some small pads 4x4 or 5x5 and always gently immerse them in boiling water for ten minutes. They can be served with butter and sage or with a good tomato sauce.

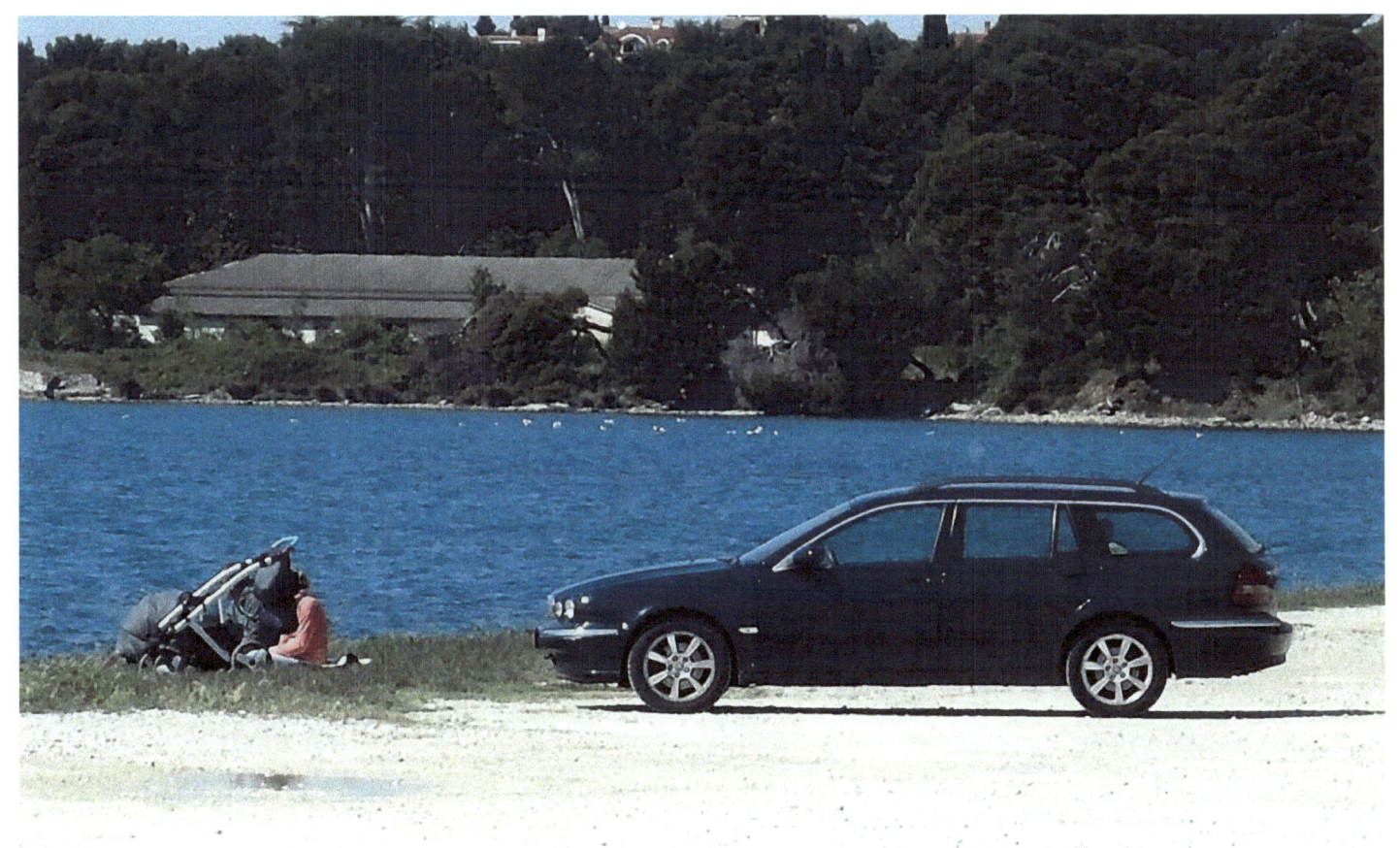

Pula

Peka, roast dish that is prepared with meat and potatoes (and also other vegetables on choice) in a pot or a tray that is placed on the grate in the fireplace. It can be prepared with any kind of meat (calf, chicken, lamb) or fish (usually octopus). Put all ingredients except the wine in a flat round tray, put it under *cripnja* (the bell-shaped iron lid) and leave it to cook for one hour. After an hour mix the meat or octopus and the potatoes and add white wine, then cover it again with *cripnja* and allow it to cook on the embers for another half an hour. If you have the fresh octopus, better freeze it for a day, so it will be softer. Peka is served with homemade bread.

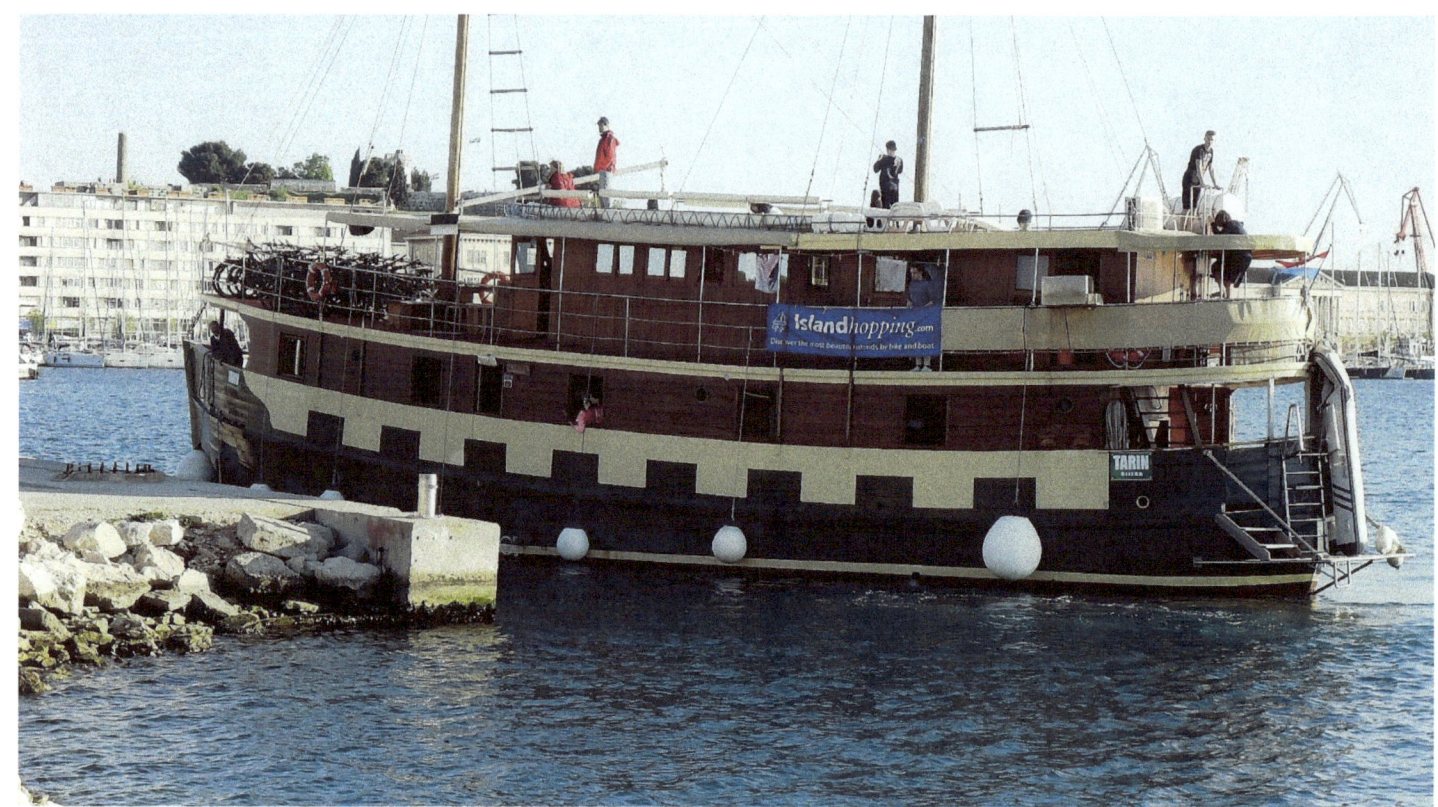

Pula

Cevapcici, mixed meatballs. Form a single dough with equal amounts of ground beef meat, of lamb and pork and half amount of well-beat lard, a finely chopped white onion, half a glass of white wine, salt and pepper. Work well the dough and make some long meatballs 6-7 cm and wide 2. Cook these meatballs on an hot grill and serve them in table with crude sliced raw onion and abundant ajvar sauce.

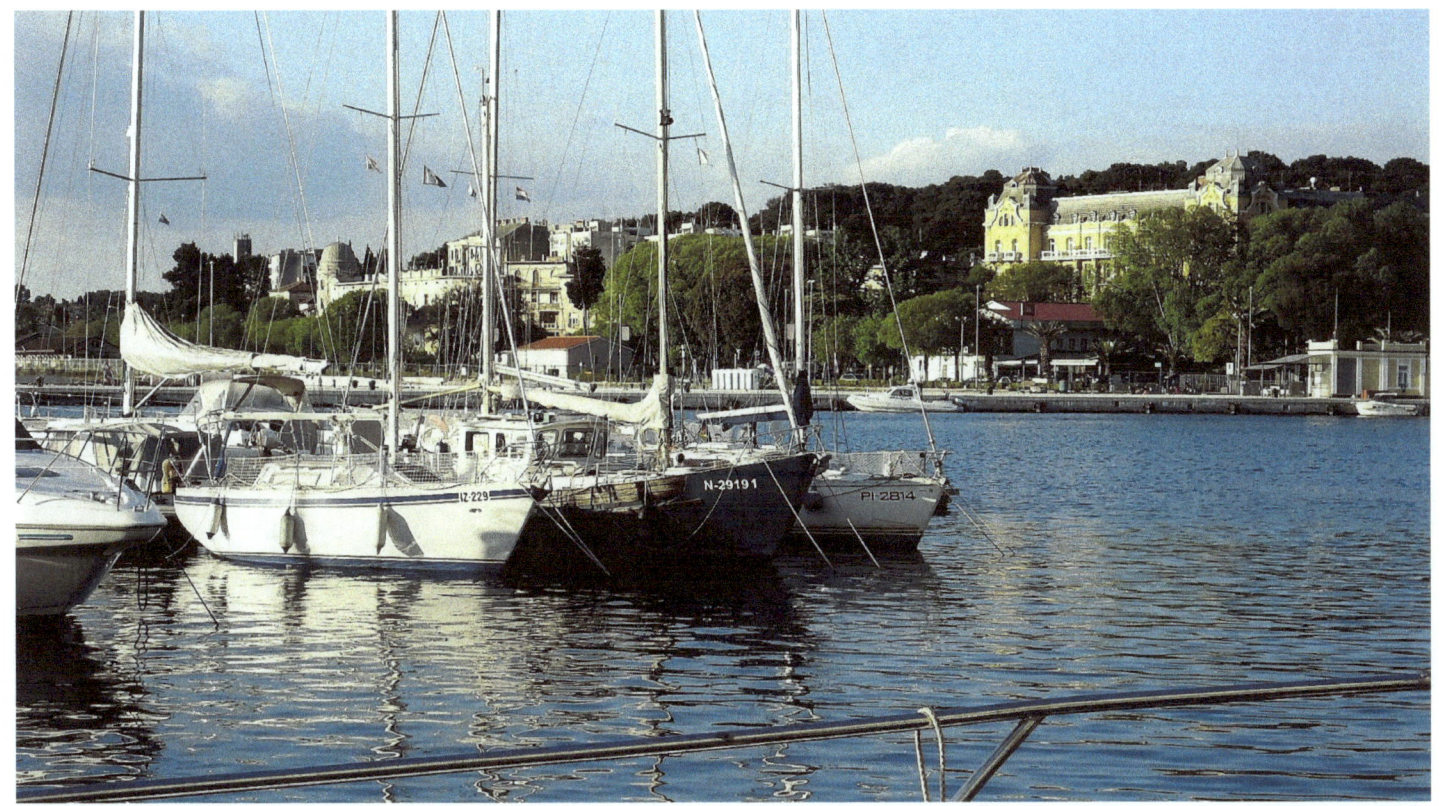

Pula

Sarma, stuffed cabbage rolls. Lightly cook the cabbage leaves in boiling water and drain them. Mix the egg with minced pork, onion chopped, thyme, paprika, salt and pepper. Distribute the compound on the cabbage leaves that will be closed as a roulade and fastened with twine. Cook the rolls with little oil in a covered pot together with the previously cooked cabbage. Season with salt and pepper and flavour with a pinch of sugar. Place everything in a bowl, sprinkle yogurt and serve with sliced tomatoes.

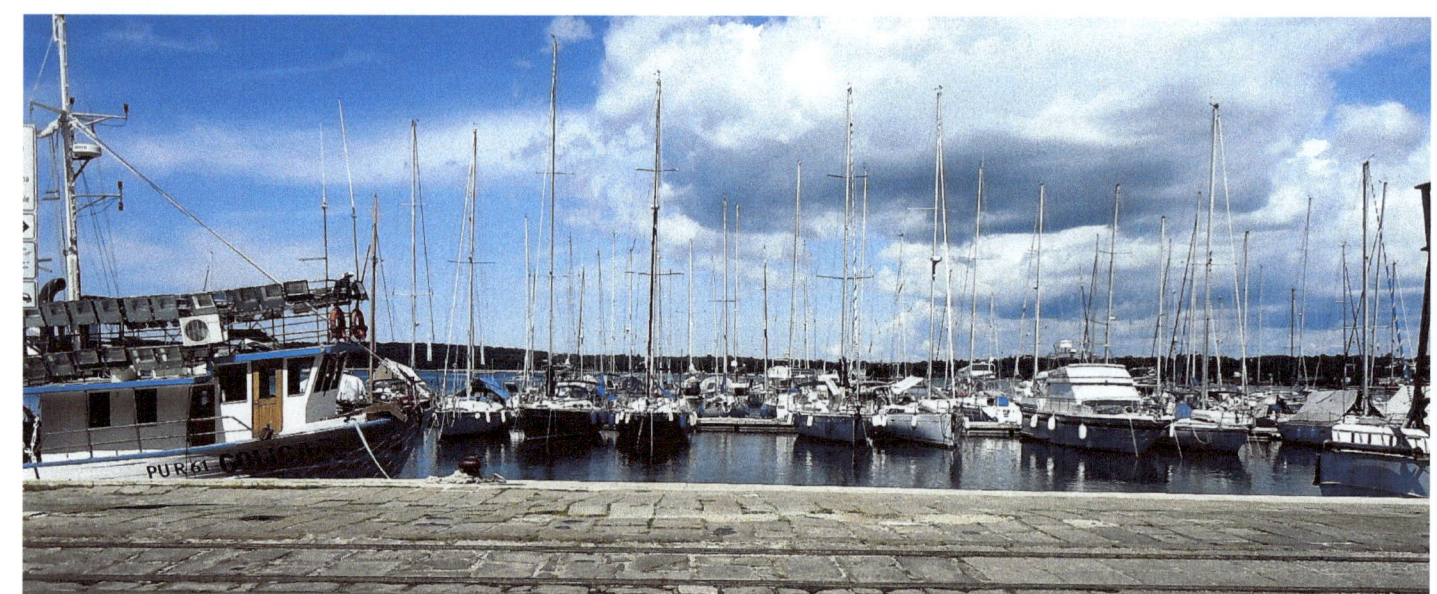

Pula

Bacalar, blitva i krumpira, codfish, chards and potatoes. Clean the cod, peel the potatoes and wash the chards. Salt the codfish, put it well in the flour and fry in the sunflower oil. Boil the cut potatoes and when they are half cooked add the chards. When the potatoes and chards are cooked, drain and fry them in olive oil, salt and pepper.

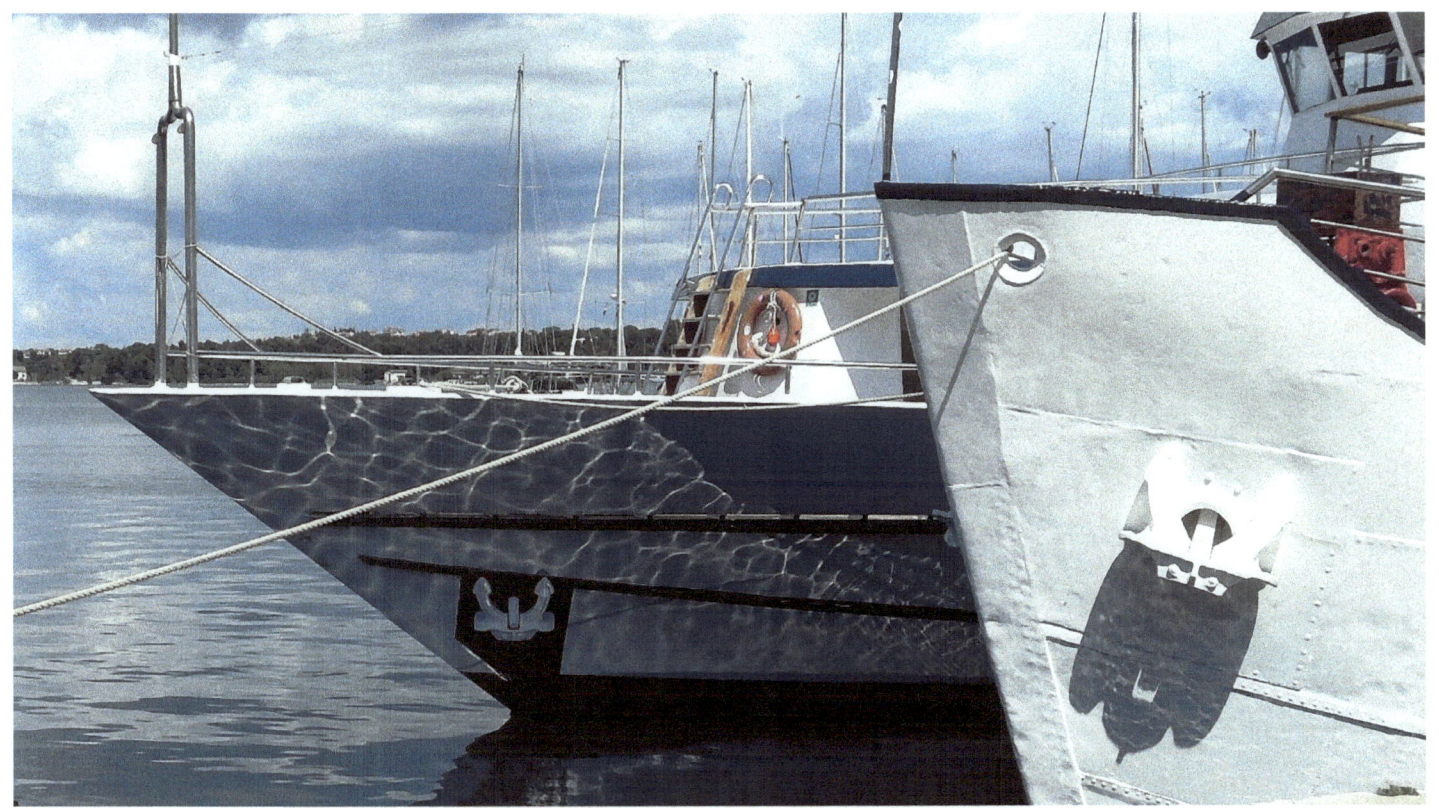

Pula

Bacalar Istarska, Istrian codfish. In a pan of oil, brown the onion with the garlic for two minutes, then combine the pieces of cod and a tablespoon of parsley. After a little, wet with a water ladle and continue cooking for five minutes. Remove the cod and add a tablespoon of minced capers, anchovy fillets in oil, grated potato and a small amount of water. After a while, merge the cod again at vivid flame, salt, reduce the flame and turn it off after fifteen minutes. Serve the cod with the sauce and, if desired, a sprinkle of lemon.

31

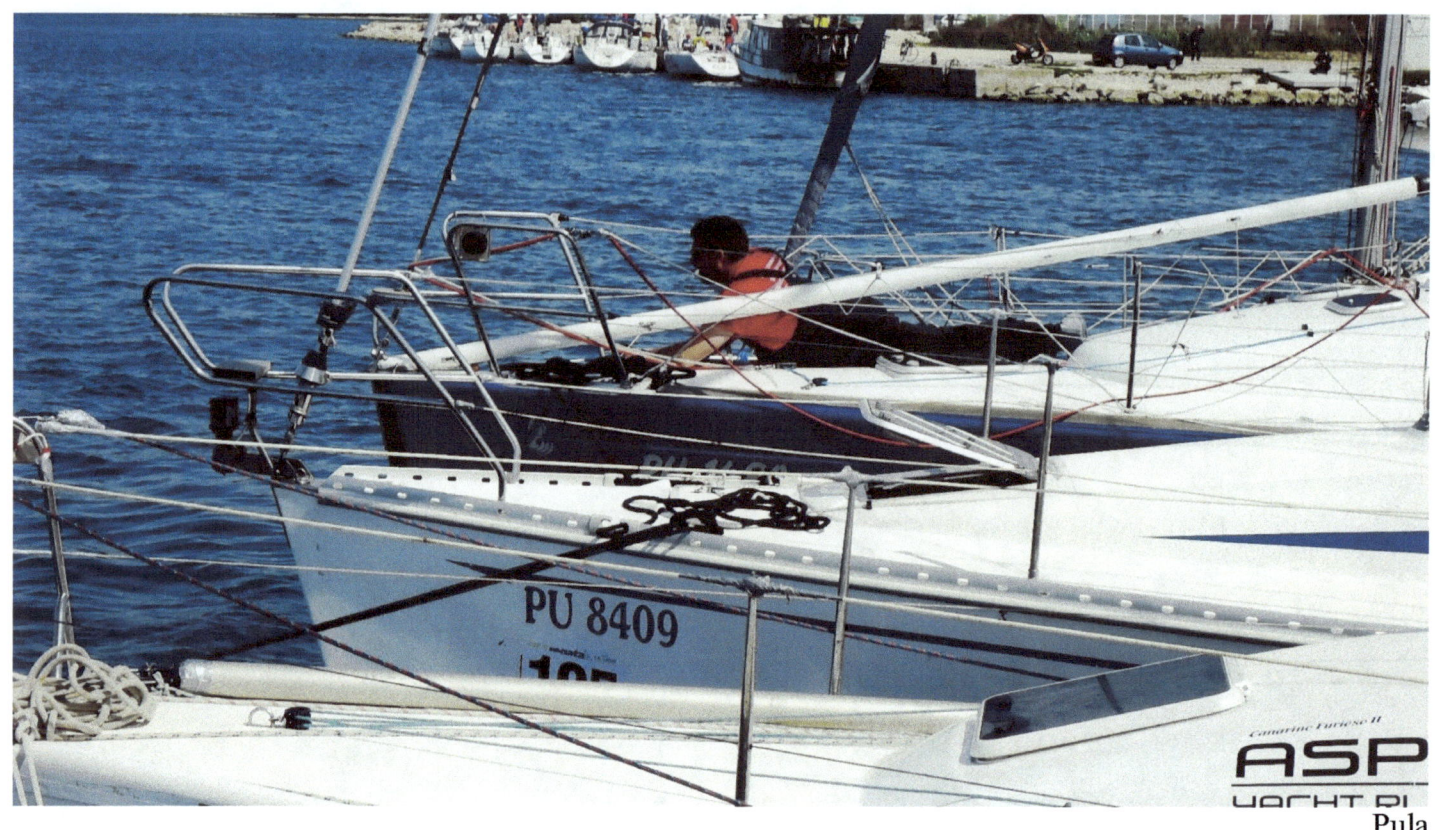

Pula

Bakalar sa krumpira, stockfish with potatoes. Cook the cod and after a while change the water. When it becomes soft, clean it and remove all spines. Brown the onion in olive oil, add the cod, cook for a while and add garlic, bay leaves, salt, pepper, tomato concentrate, parsley, white wine and a little water. Clean the potatoes, cut into slices and let boil in salted water for 10 minutes. Take off a little water from the potatoes and add the stockfish. Cook until the potatoes are cooked. Add salt and pepper to taste.

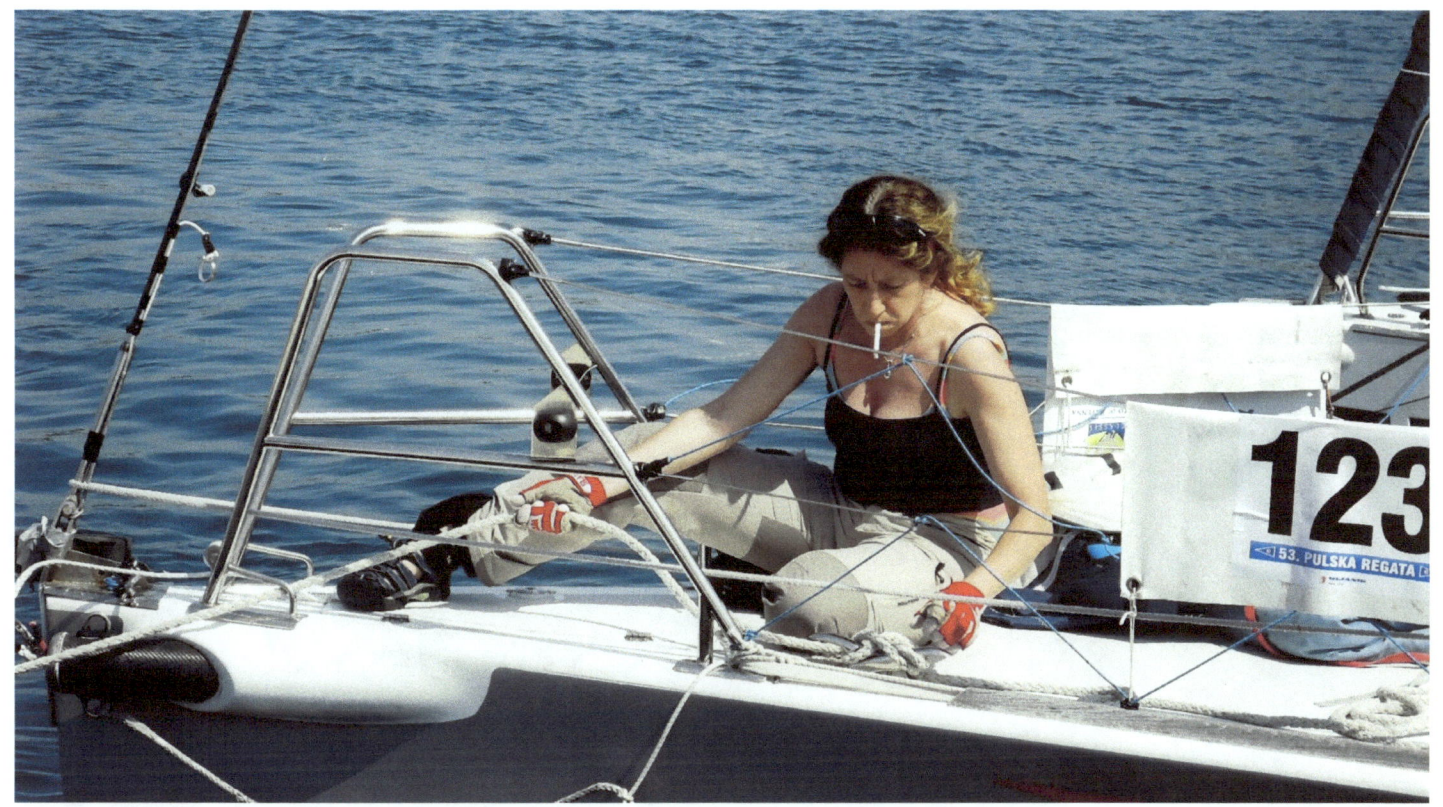

Pula

Brancin s punjenjem, sea bass with filling. Clean the fish, cut off its head, separate the meat from the fishbone, sprinkle a little lemon juice. Prepare the filling with finely chopped anchovies, pitted olives, pine nuts, basil and olive oil. Fill the fish with filling and close the two filets. Salt, add pepper, oil and pass it in the grated bread. Place it in the baking pan with olive oil and cook it in the oven at 180 degrees. Once in a while add fish broth and white wine.

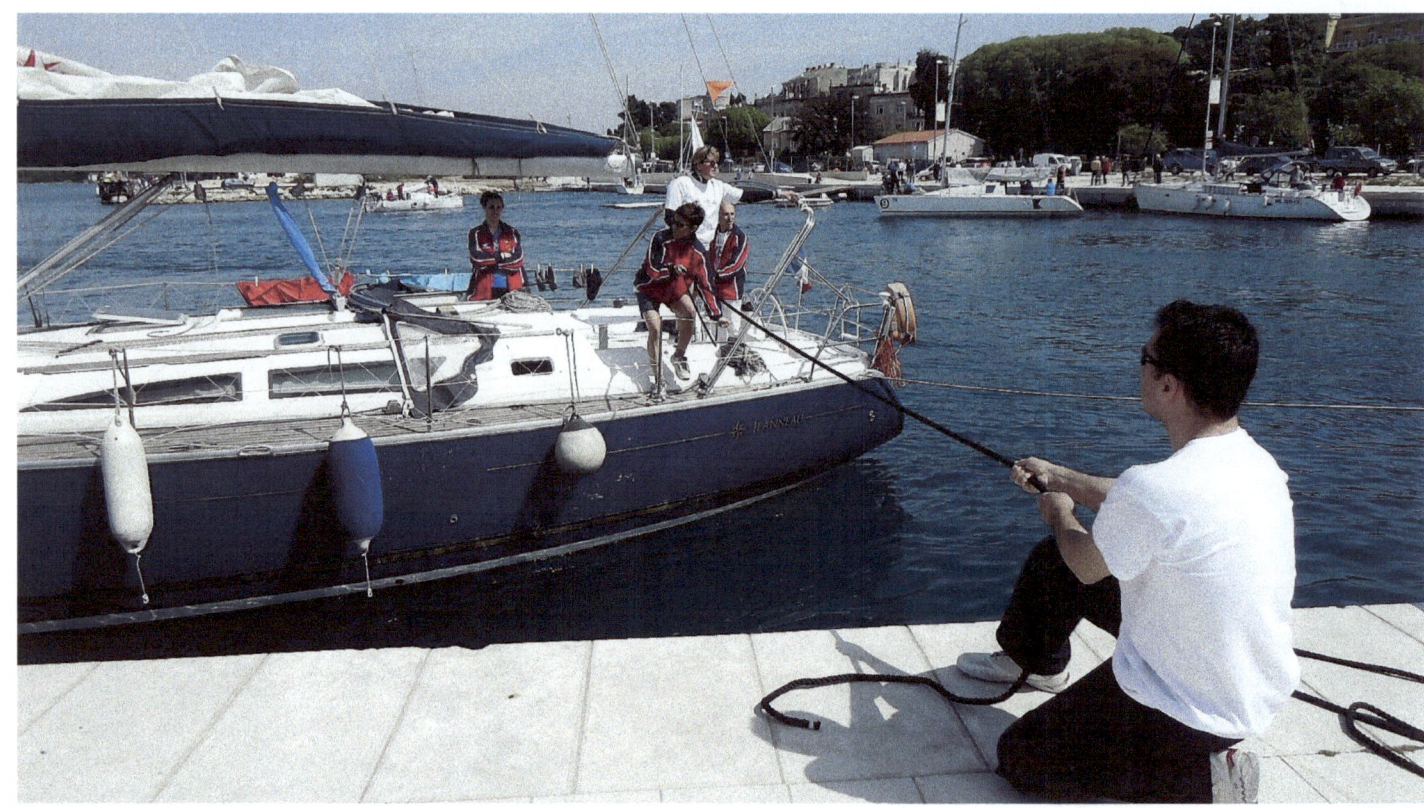

Pula

Dagnje Busara, mussels at the busara. Carefully clean the mussels, then peel and chop the garlic and parsley. In a large saucepan, heat the oil, add garlic and mix quickly. Pour a spoonful of breadcrumbs, parsley, wine and bring to a boil. Add the mussels and sprinkle with other parsley. Cover the saucepan and cook on high flame for 10 minutes. Shake the saucepan a couple of times during cooking. Put the mussels in a hot dish. Add again breadcrumbs in the sauce in pot and cook two minutes, then pour the sauce over the mussels.

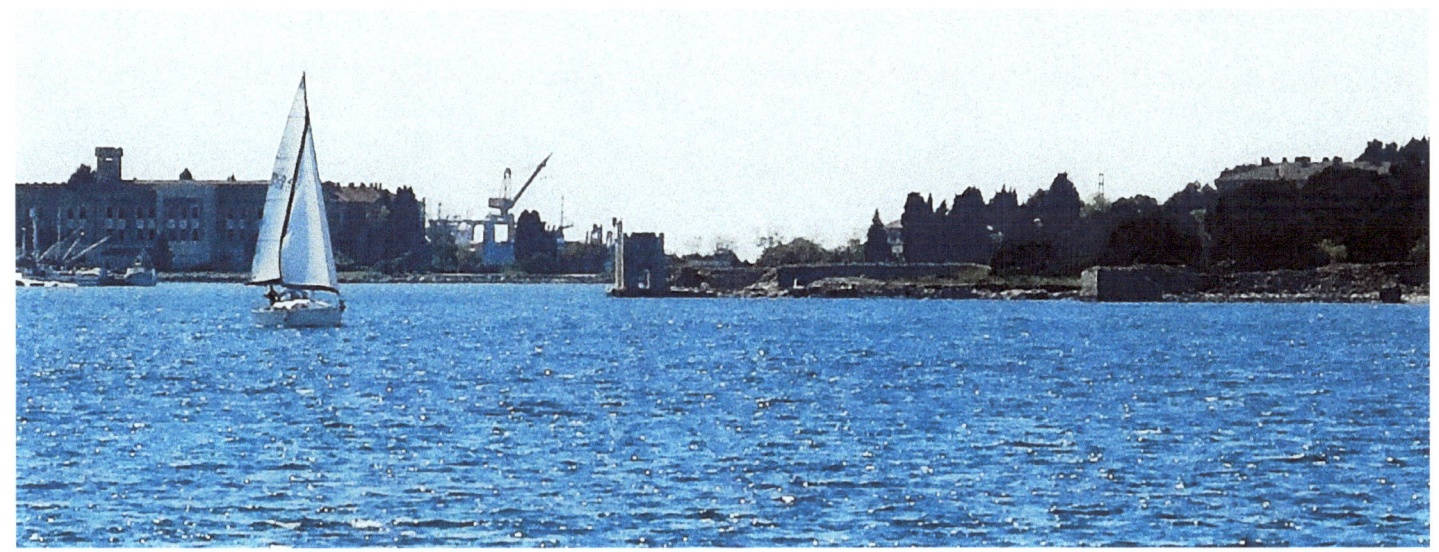

Pula

Gulaš od lignje s palentom, squids broth with polenta. Clean the squids, be careful not to break the bag containing the serum (put it aside), cut an onion into small pieces and brown until it becomes golden. Add the squids, two cloves of finely chopped garlic, salt, pepper, a little parsley and red wine. Cook for about 15 minutes and accompany the dish with polenta.

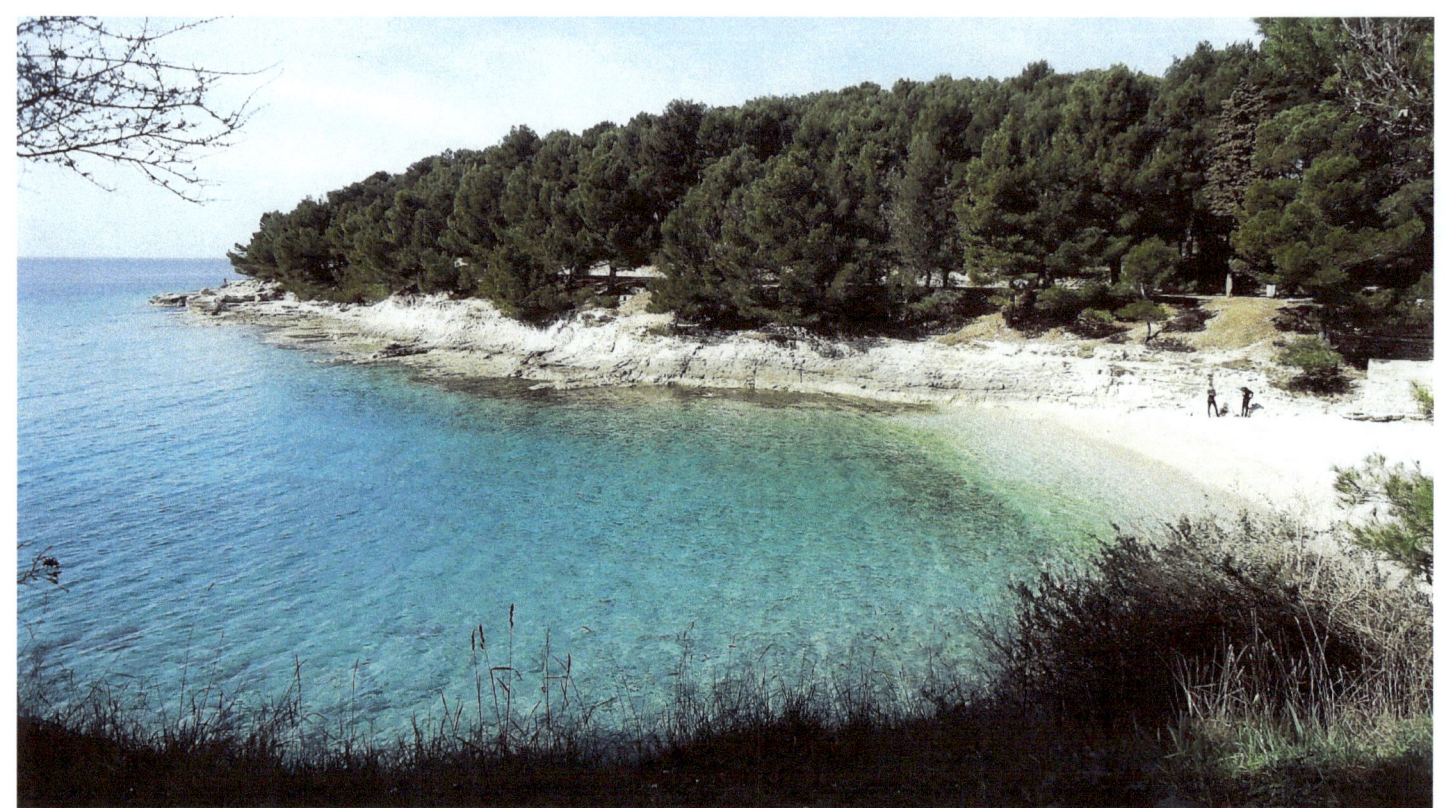

Pula

Sipe s blitvom i palentom, cuttlefish with chards and polenta. Soak in the olive oil the sliced onion, the crushed garlic and the parsley. Add the cuttlefish clean, washed and cut into small pieces. Cook slowly until the cuttlefish soften. Add water every now and then add the washed and cut chards, salt, pepper and cook slowly to soften the chards. Add water if necessary to get a dense dish at the right point.

Cook the polenta in a saucepan for at least half an hour as follows: in boiling salty water pour a bit corn flour, mix, pour the rest of the flour and cook by mixing with a wooden big ladle. Just before the end of cooking add a teaspoon of olive oil (or grease). The polenta does not have to be too hard. When the polenta is cooked pour it into a large wood dish, drilling a hole in the middle. Pour over the cuttlefish with the chards and let the polenta absorb a bit, then serve.

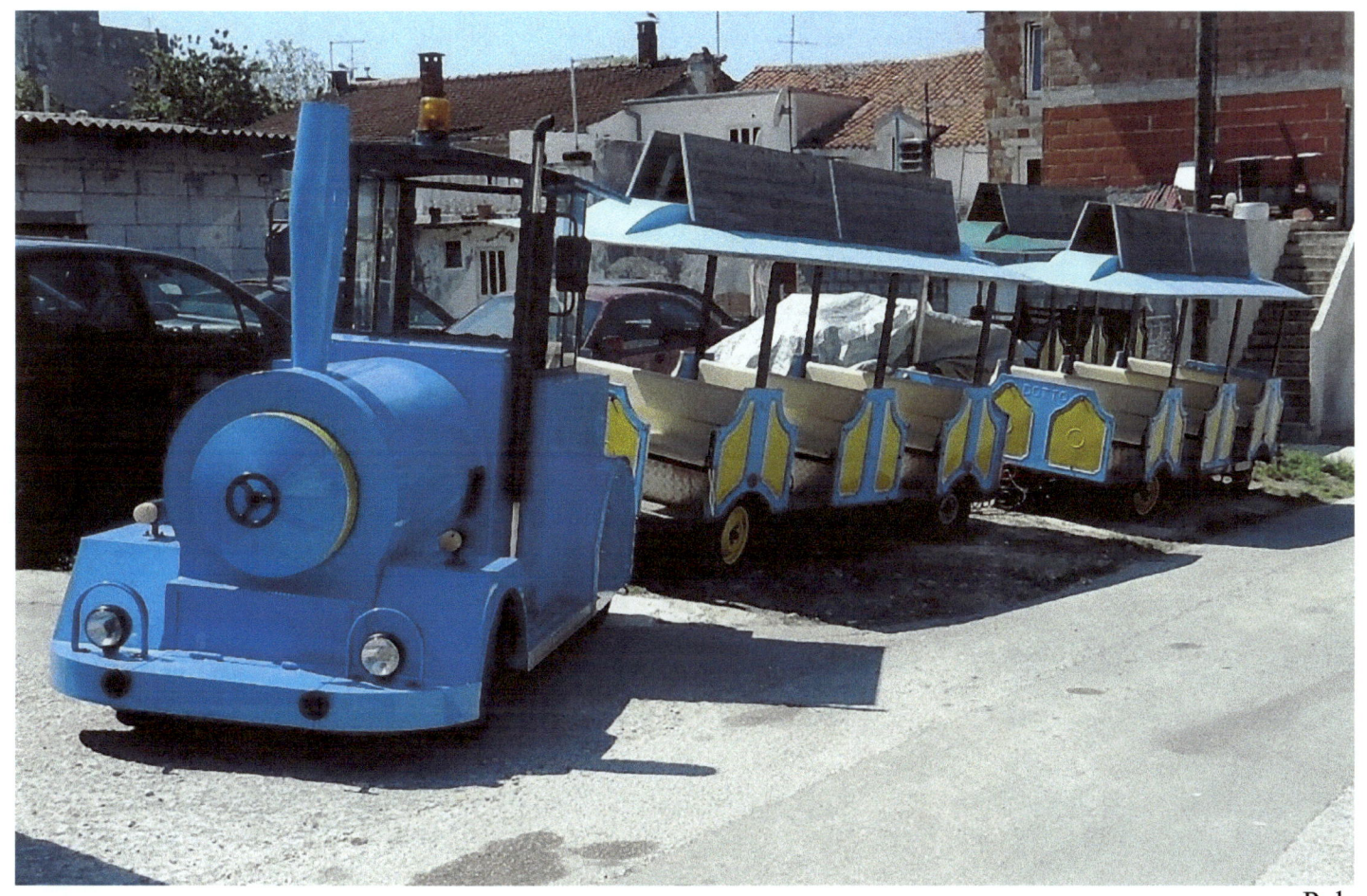

Pula

Lignje punjene crvenom cikorije, squids stuffed with red radicchio. Clean and wash the squids. Prepare the filling with raw ham, garlic, salt and pepper. Cook it with half a glass of olive oil. Place the chilled filling on a red radicchio leaf, close it and put in the squid using a toothpick. Cook the squids stuffed at medium heat in a pan with olive oil.

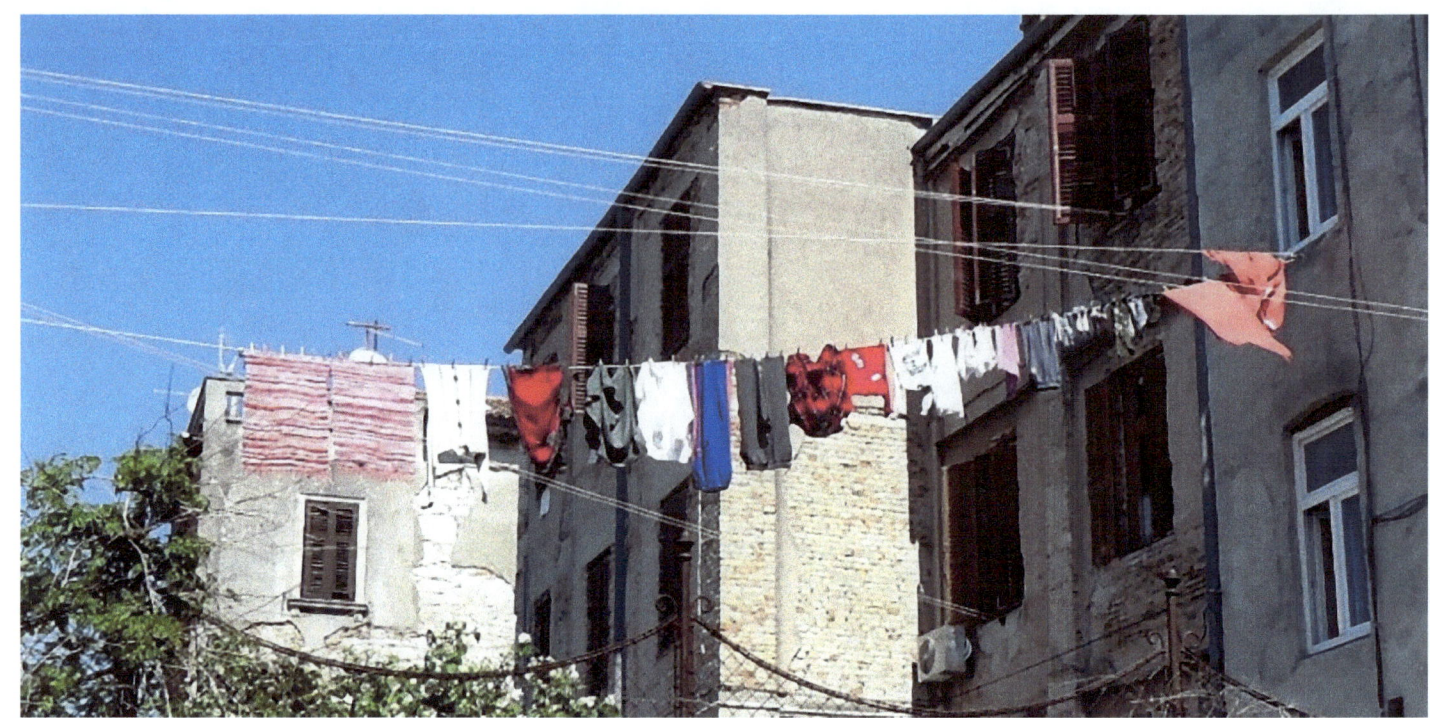

Pula

Lignje s krumpira, squids with potatoes. Clean, wash and slice squids in two cm wide strips. Peel and slice finely potatoes. Chop up the garlic and the parsley. Pour a little oil into a frying pan, place a layer of potatoes and salt. Then put the squids sliced over the potatoes, add garlic, parsley, pepper and other spices of your taste. Finally, cover with the remaining potatoes. A splash of parsley, salt and a little oil. Cover the pot and cook in oven at 220 ° C for about 45 minutes.

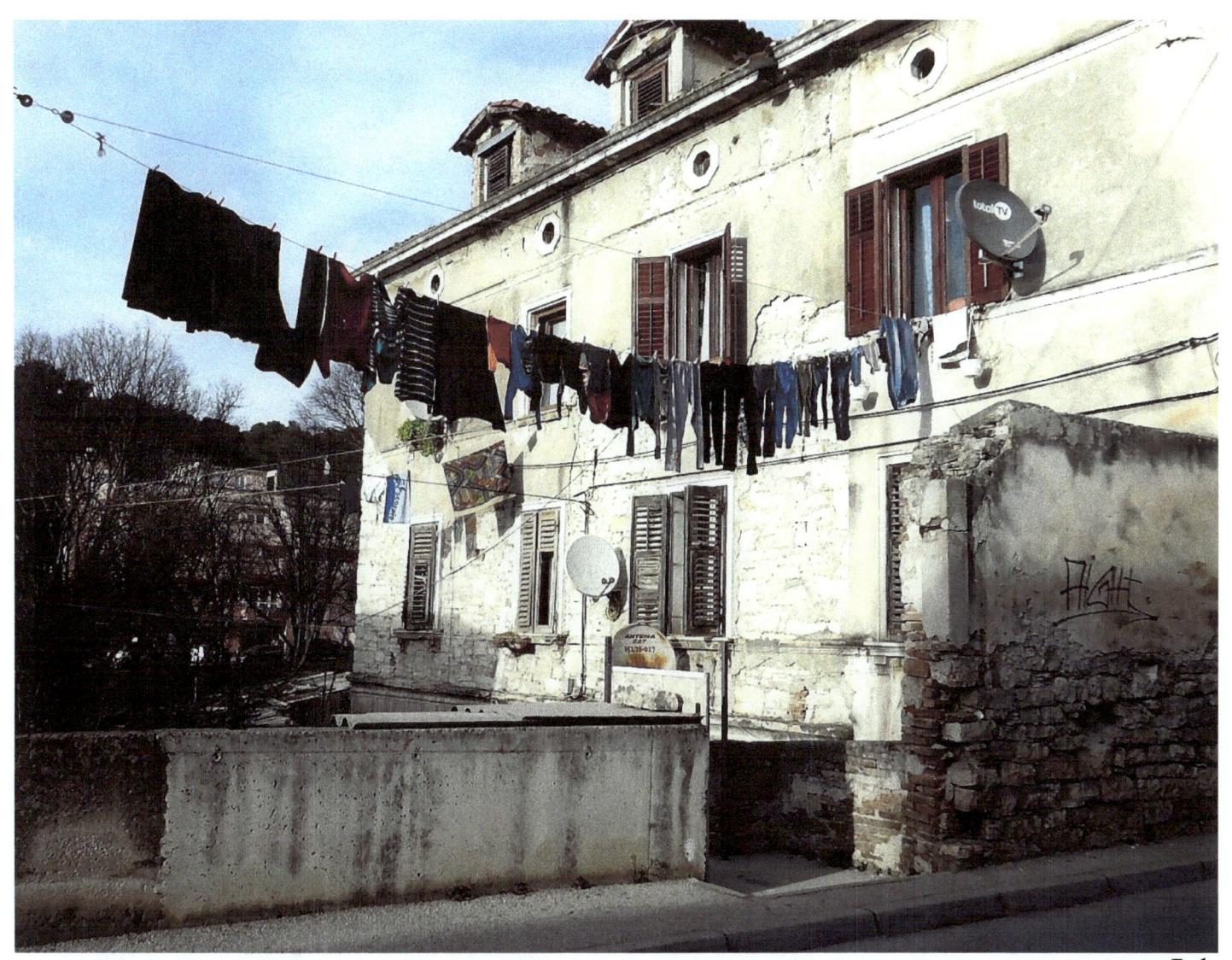

Pula

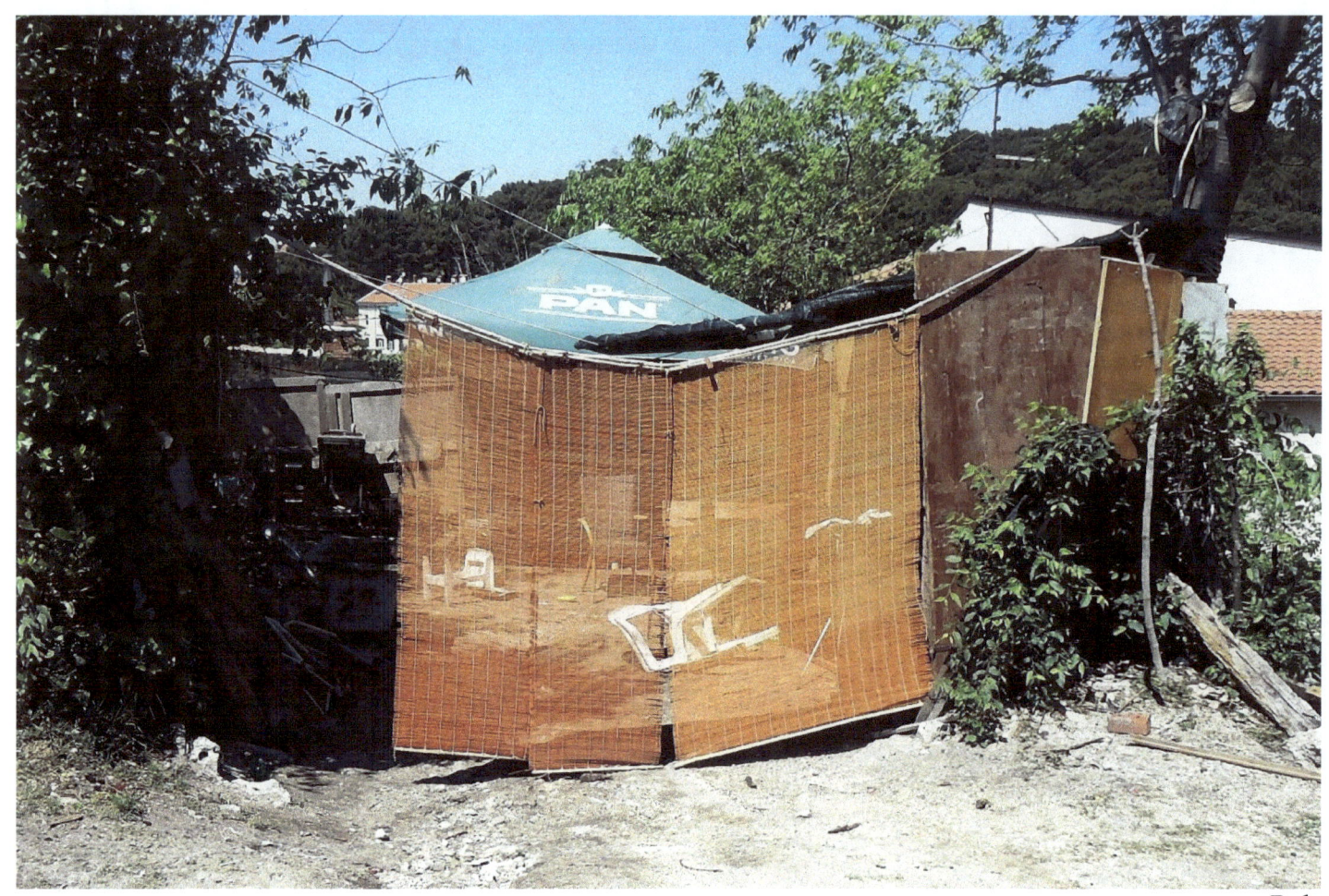

Pula

Škampi na buzaru, scampi at the busara. Jump the scampi with sweet onions, garlic, olive oil, wine and a lot of chopped parsley. The sauce you get is called busara. The recipe is very simple: the real secret is the delicious Kvarner scampi, to be cooked whole (but there are also versions with the only meat) after having fried garlic, chili pepper and breadcrumbs in extra virgin olive oil. Then pour the white wine and combine the peeled tomatoes, with the addition of parsley when baking is accomplish.

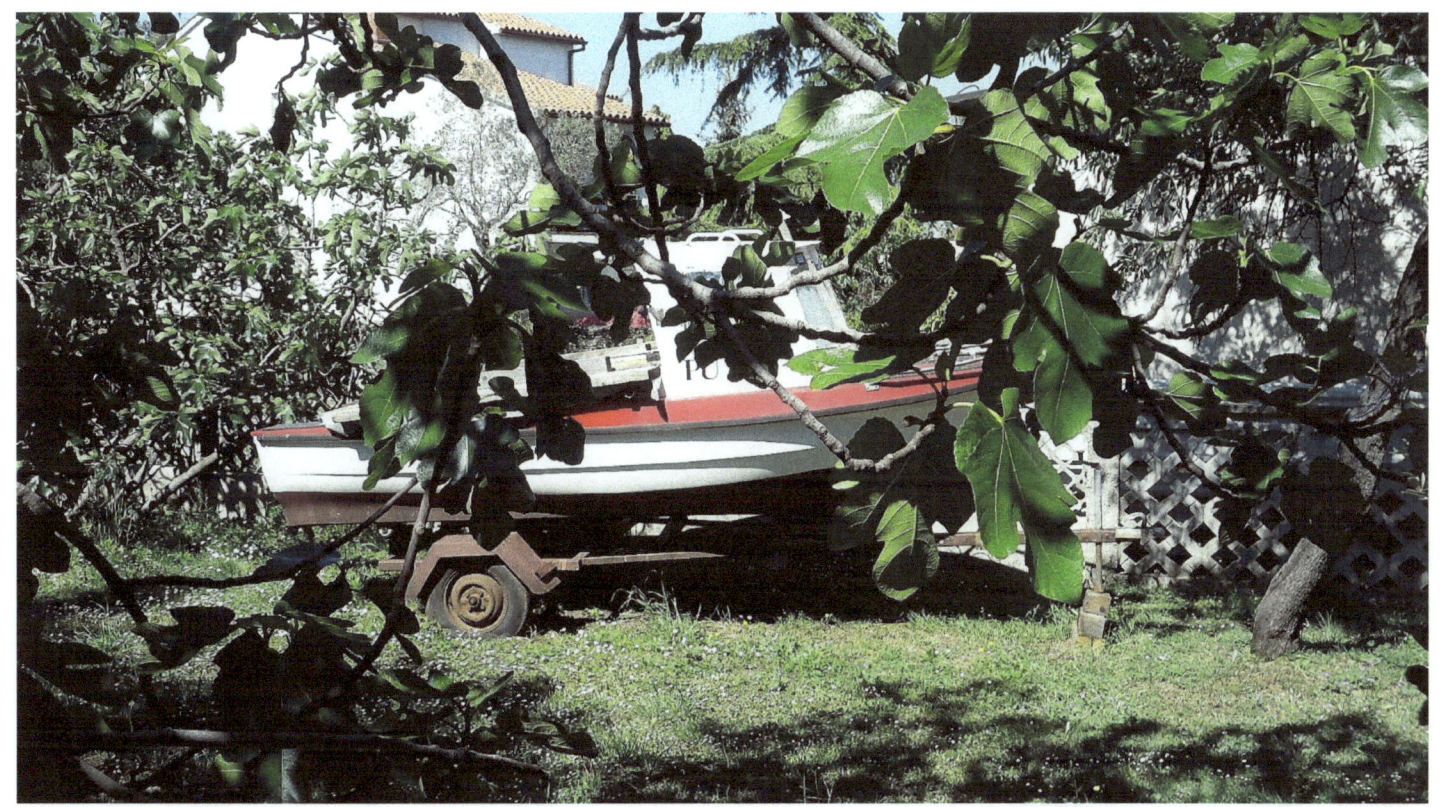

Stinjan (Pula)

Srdele s lukom, sardines with onions. Flour the sardines and fry them in olive oil. When they are well fried, place them in a deep dish or another container (better than clay, never metal!). On the remaining oil, fry the sliced onion, crushed garlic, add the laurel leaf, rosemary, salt and pepper, mix and add a glass of malvasia and vinegar. Boil and then let evaporate a bit. When finished, pour it over the sardines to cover them. Put in the fridge and let rest for a while (even a few days). Serve with bread or polenta.

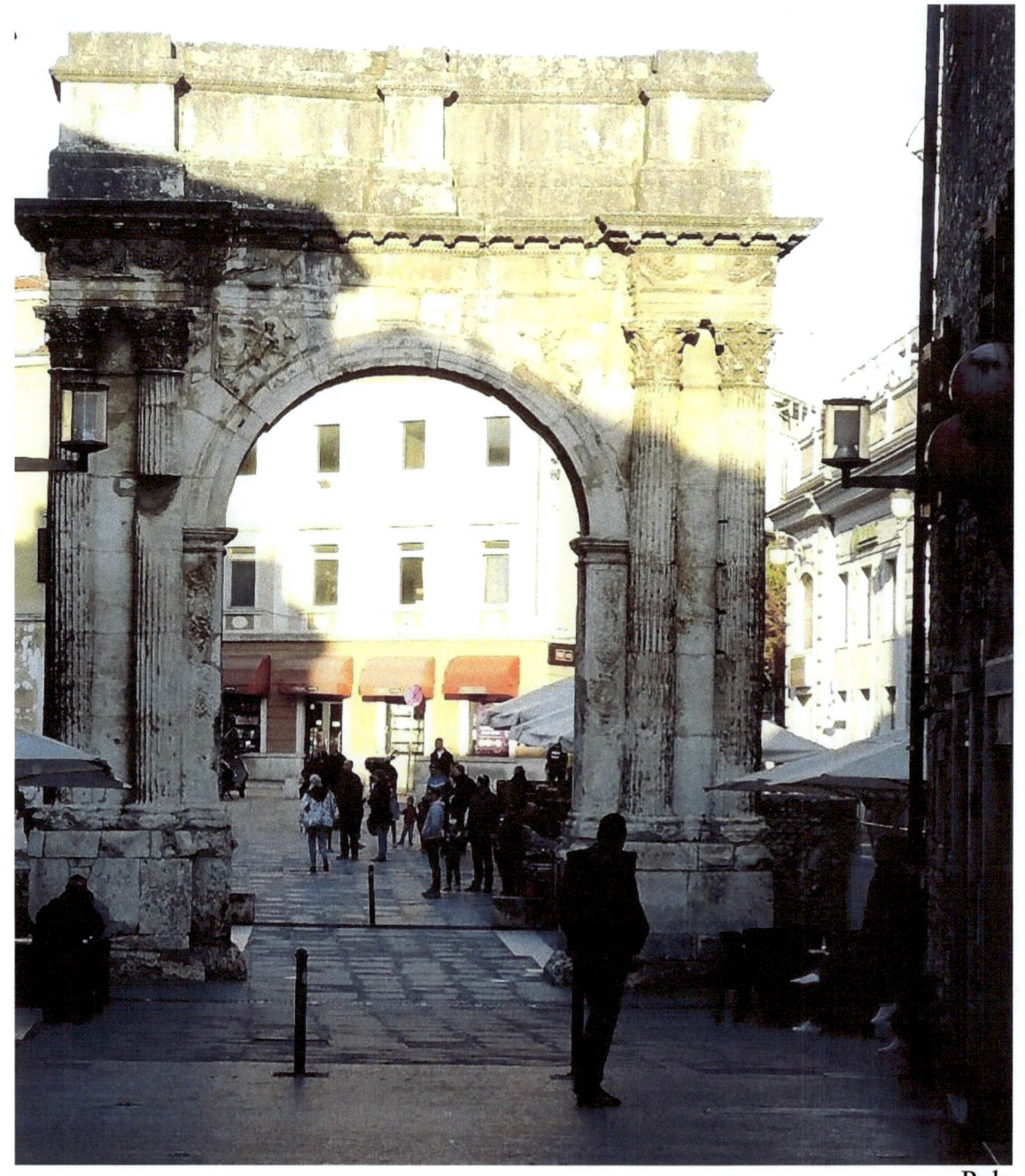

Pula

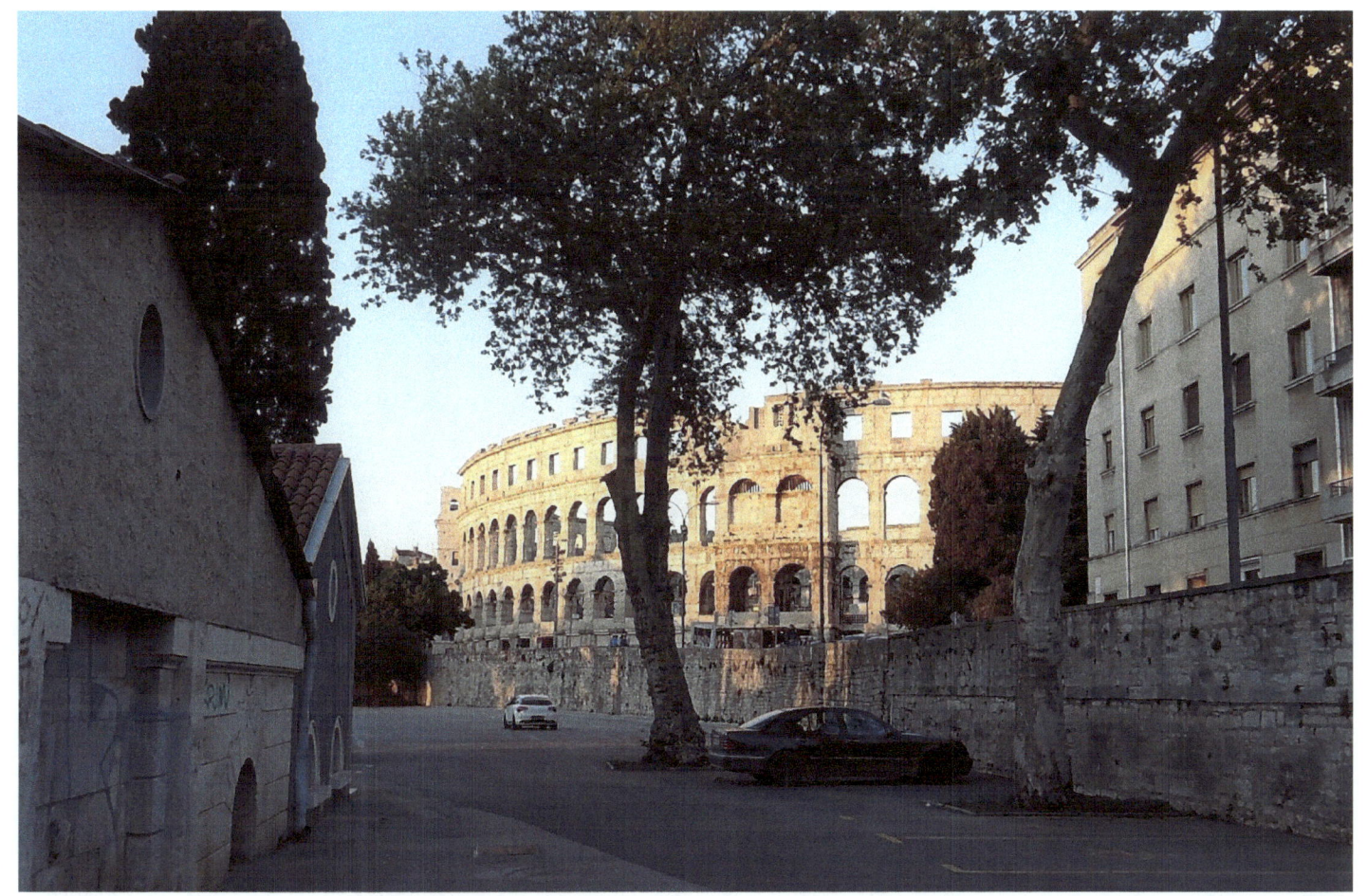

Pula

Fritaja s divljim šparogama, omelette with wild asparagus. Fry small pieces asparagus in olive oil. Add on several occasions hot water until to soften asparagus. Pour the eggs beaten with salt and pepper. Mix well and when the eggs coagulate remove them from fire and serve with polenta. Fry small pieces bacon in olive oil (or sausages), pour them on the omelette and serve with the bread.

43

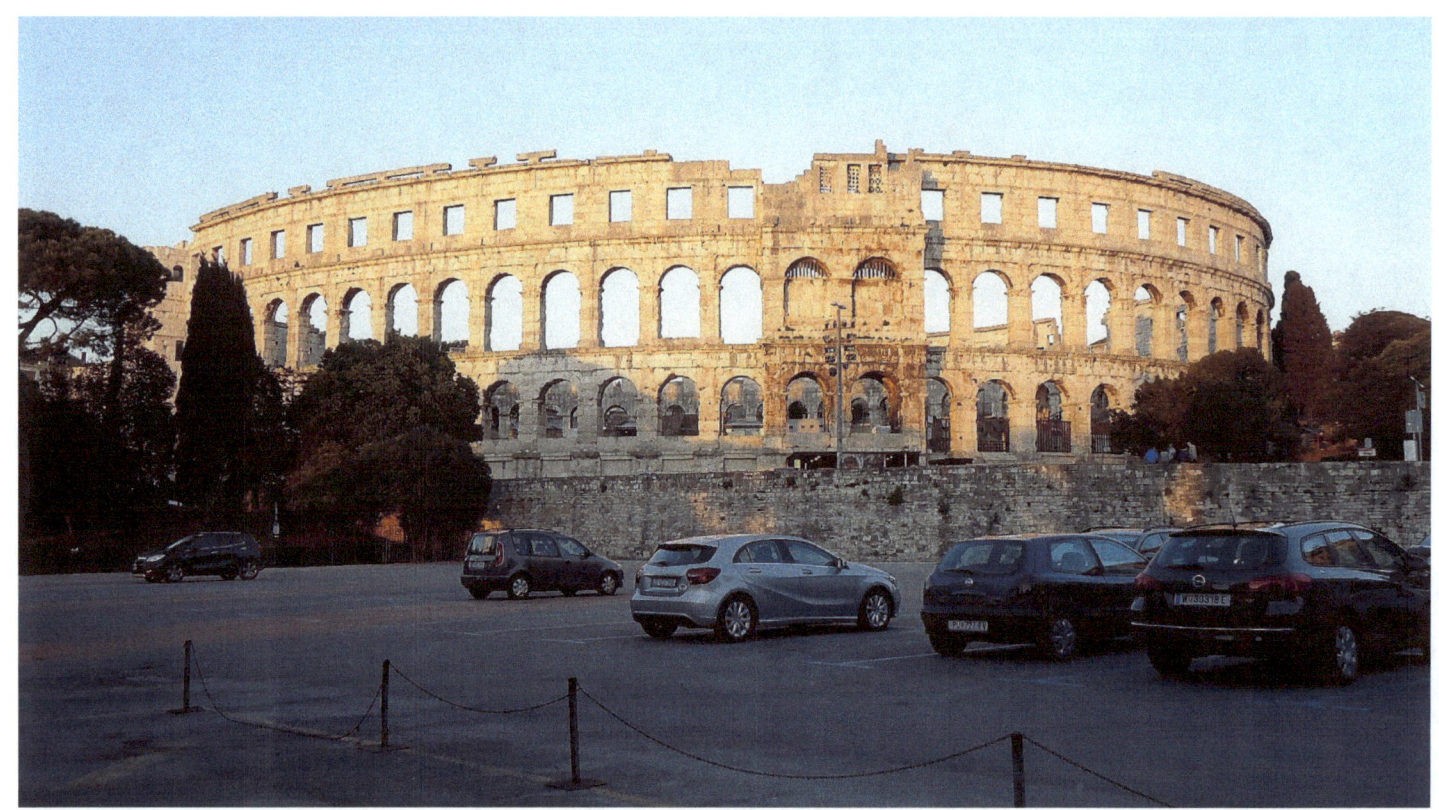

Pula

Punjene artičoke, stuffed artichokes. Open the artichokes clean and with the cut tips. Fill with the stuffing by grated bread, parsley and crushed garlic, salt and pepper. Arrange the artichokes in a pan with olive oil, add water to cover about 3/4 of height of the artichokes and cook in the pan covered on medium flame until the artichokes are soft. Serve with polenta.

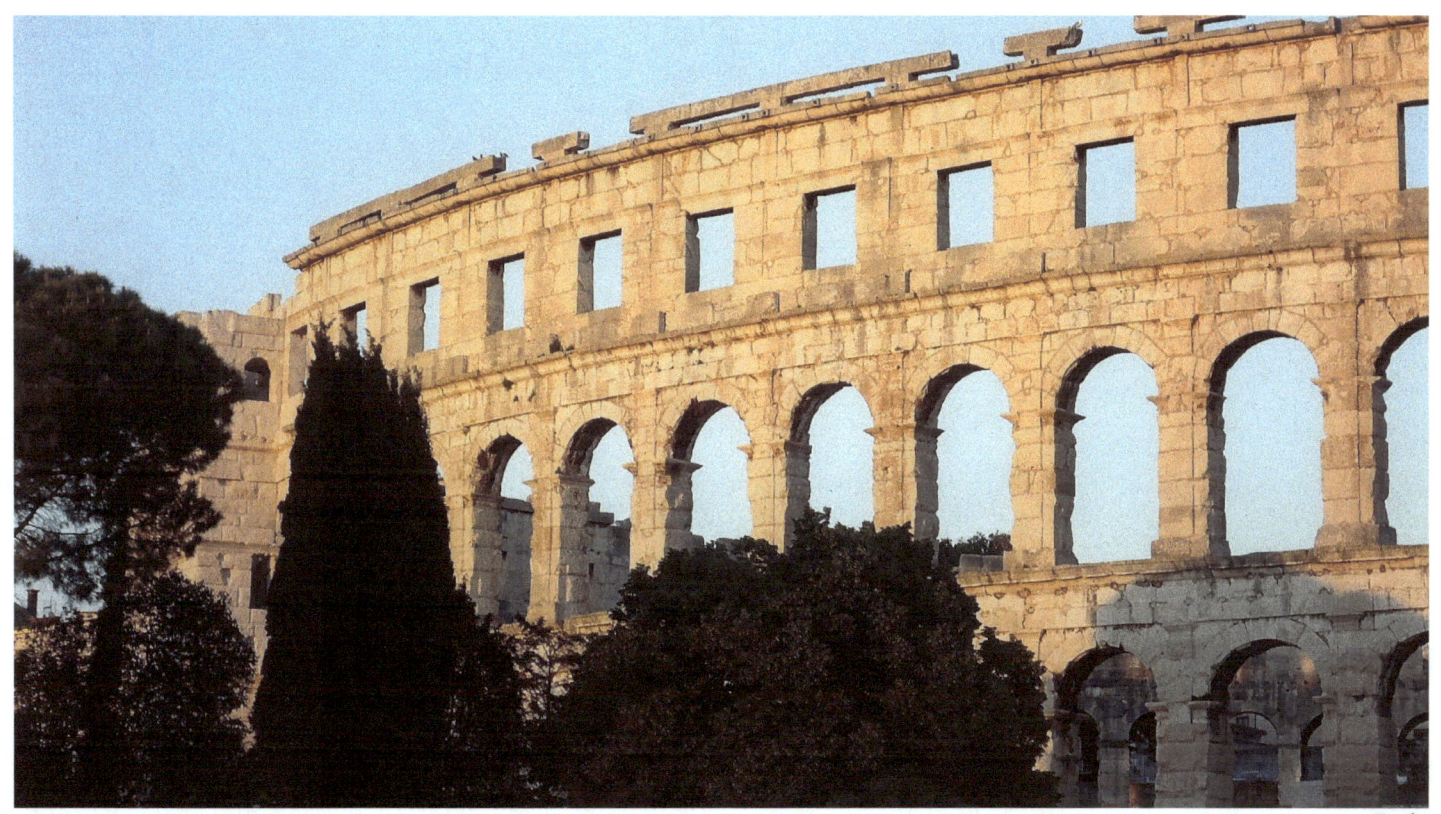

Pula

Griški kres, sweet with nuts and dried figs. Mix milk, cream, sugar and dip there the slices of sweet bread. Grease the pan and place the bread. Grate half the apples, crumble the nuts and figs, put together cinnamon, honey, rum and yolks previously beaten. Mix well and pour on the bread. Remove the core to the remained apples, cut them into disks and let them boil in sugared water. When they become soft, drain and hand out them over the sweet. Beat well two eggs with sugar, pour them over the apples and put everything in the oven. Work well with a bit sugar, remove the pan from the oven and pour over the apples. Put everything in the oven at 180 degrees until it becomes golden.

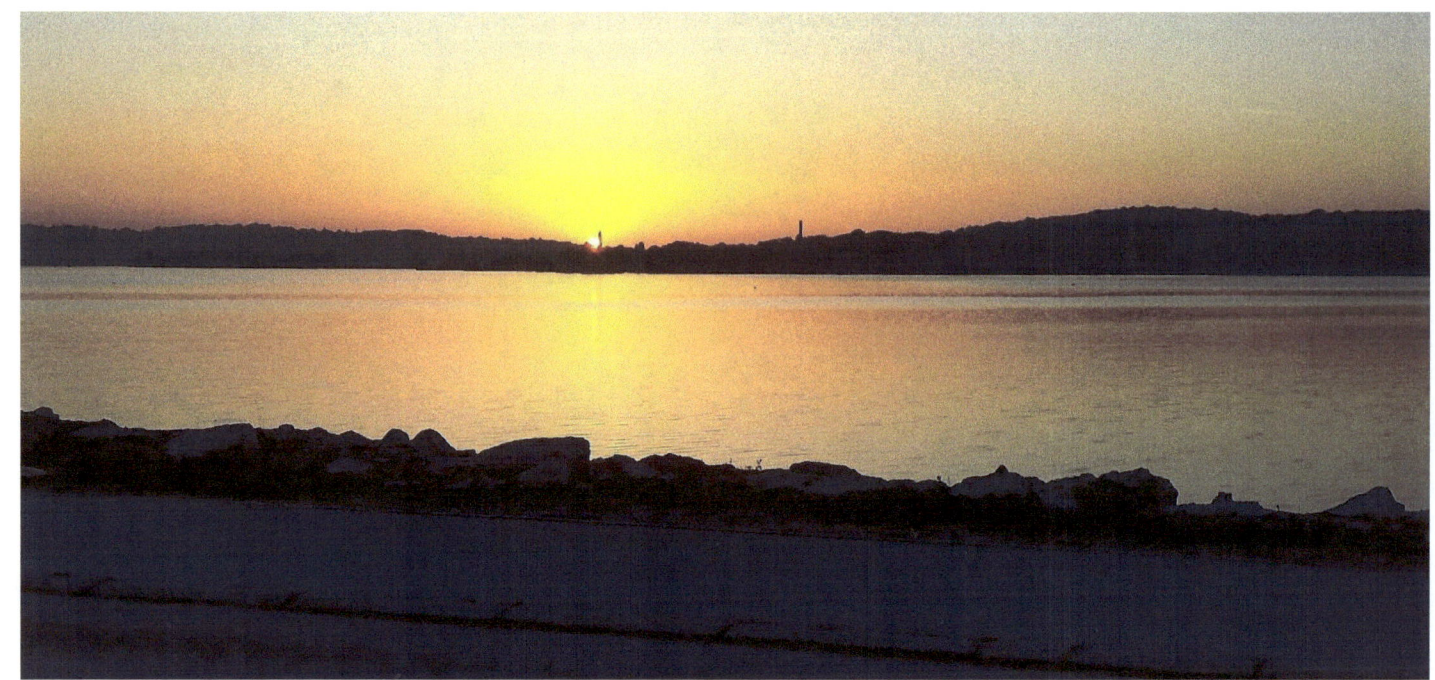

Pula

Krumpir i blitva, potatoes and chards. *Blitva* or chard is a "cousin" of spinach prepared with potatoes, garlic and olive oil. Wash the potatoes, immerse them in a pot of cold water without peeling and make to boil. Clean and wash the chards, boil them in plenty of salty boiling water and when soft (it will take only a few minutes) drain them and pour immediately under a cold water jet. This will conserve a brighter green color. Peel the potatoes still hot, cut into chunks and crush roughly with a fork. Chop the well-dripped chards with a sharp knife. Fry in a little oil two crushed garlic cloves without coloring them too much. Add the potatoes and the chards and season a few minutes before serving. This dish is beautifully accompanied with grilled fish or calamari.

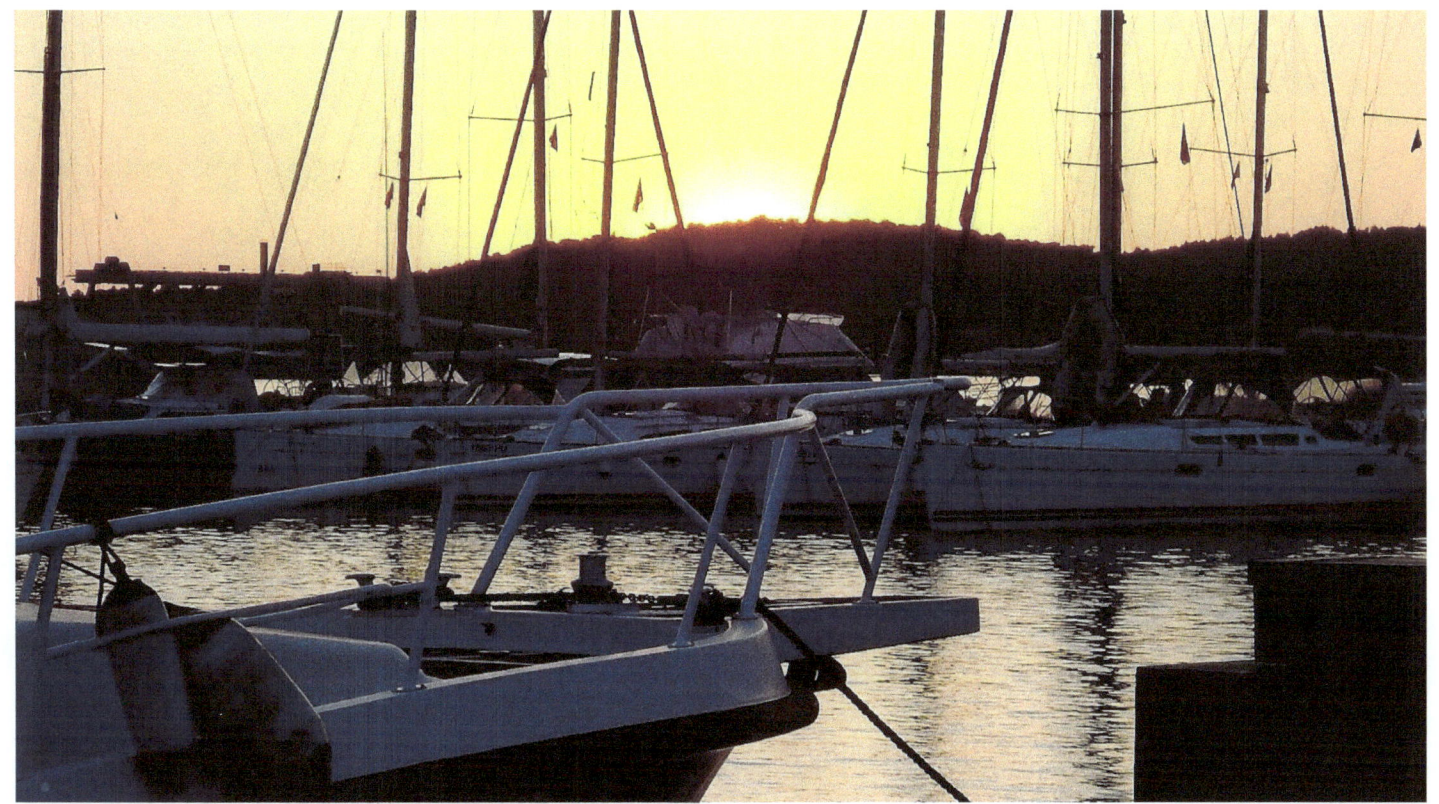

Pula

Palačinke na refoška, crepes with refosco. To prepare the dough, beat the eggs with salt and milk. Now add the refosco and flour alternately and beat until you get a dense, but liquid dough. For the stuffing fry in a frying pan the grated apples together with sugar and the cinnamon until you get a purée. The purée can also be replaced with jam (for example plum). On a few oil drops pour a little dough and fry one crepe. Fill it with stuffing and roll it up. Sprinkle with the sauce prepared by browning the breadcrumbs on the butter, to which you have added the vanilla sugar and the refosco that you have let evaporate for a few moments.

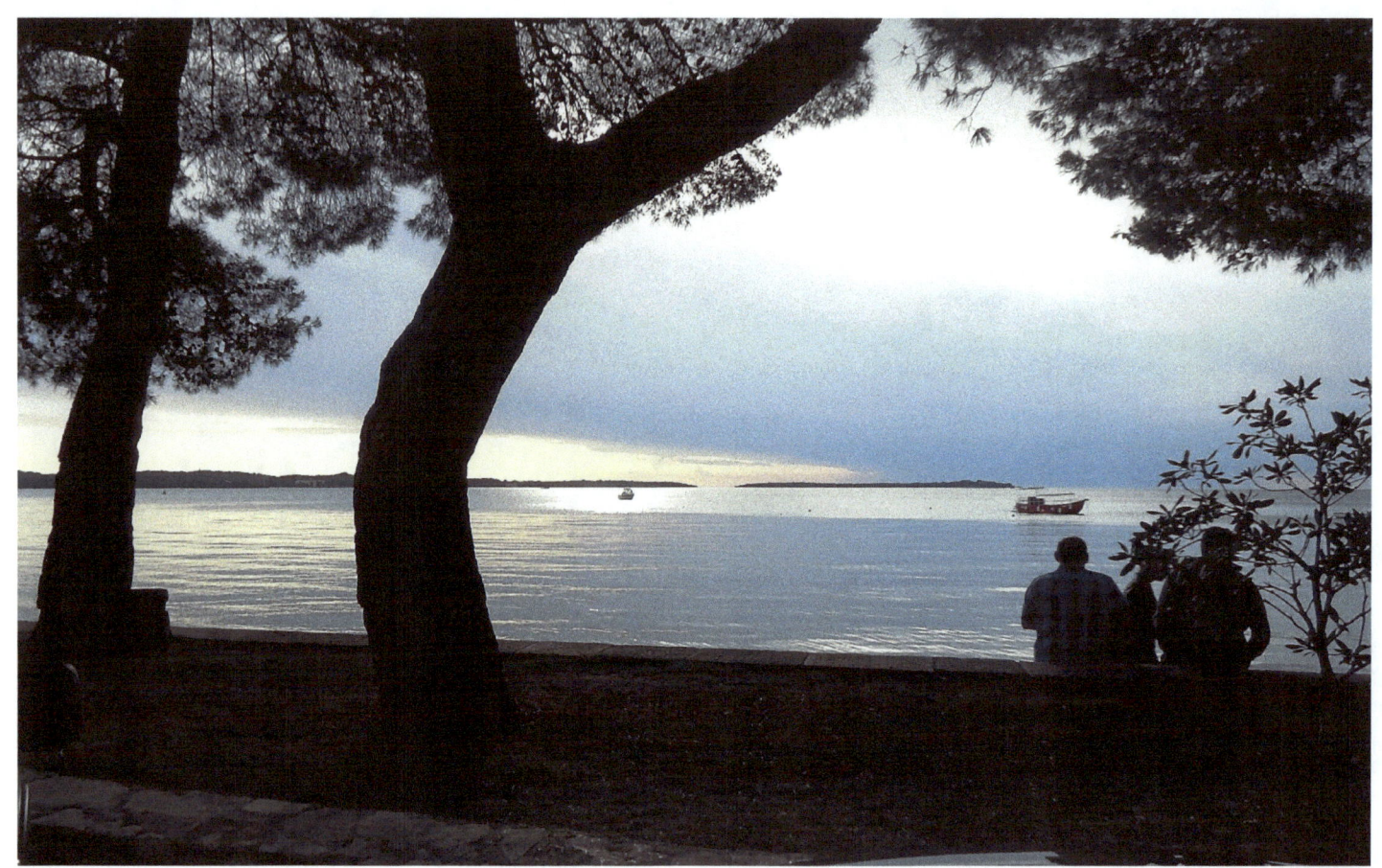

Fazana

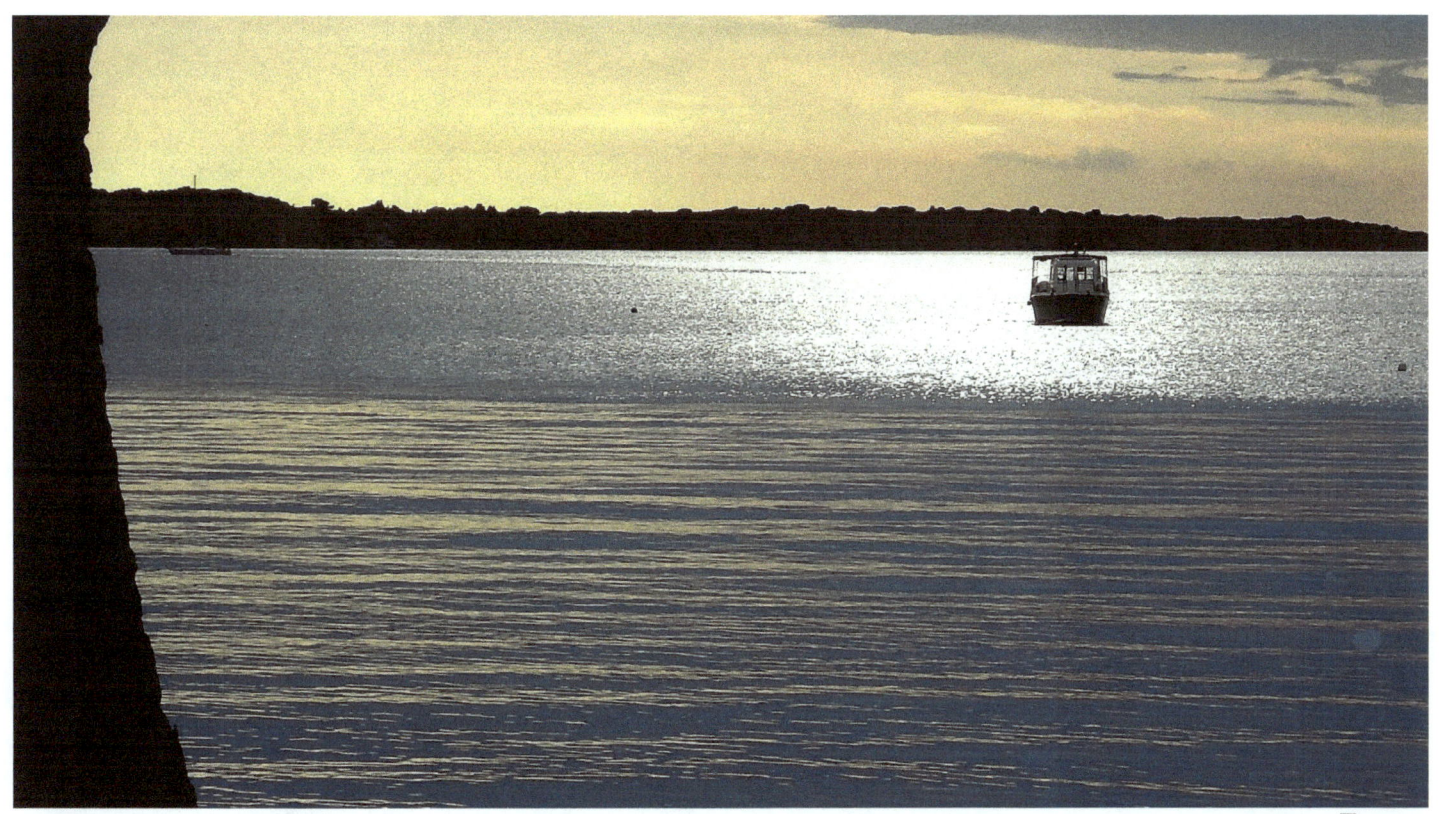

Fazana

Pinca, traditional Easter bread. The *pinca* is a very rich bread consumed at the end of Lent. Dissolve and start a spoon of beer yeast with a glass of lukewarm milk and a tablespoon of sugar, leave the mixture in a warm place until it becomes frothy. Soak the sultan raisins with rum for half an hour. In the mixing bowl, combine flour and salt, add the yeast mixture, melted butter, another glass of milk, three egg yolks, ground sugar, two spoons of vanilla sugar and the grated peels of lemon and half an orange. Mix the ingredients on medium speed until the dough begins to detach from the walls. Add the raisins and rum, reduce the speed and stir for a few more minutes until the dough is smooth and elastic. Make a ball and transfer it to an oiled bowl. Cover with transparent film and leave it in a warm place rising for two hours. After this time divide the pasta into two equal parts and mold each piece in ball form. Transfer them in a baking tray lined with baking paper and brush them with the egg banged. Let them rise for an hour, brush again with egg and leave in a warm environment for another hour. With the tip of a sharp knife, cut the surface by forming a cross and cook for 30 minutes at 180 degrees until the sweets will take a nice gilding.

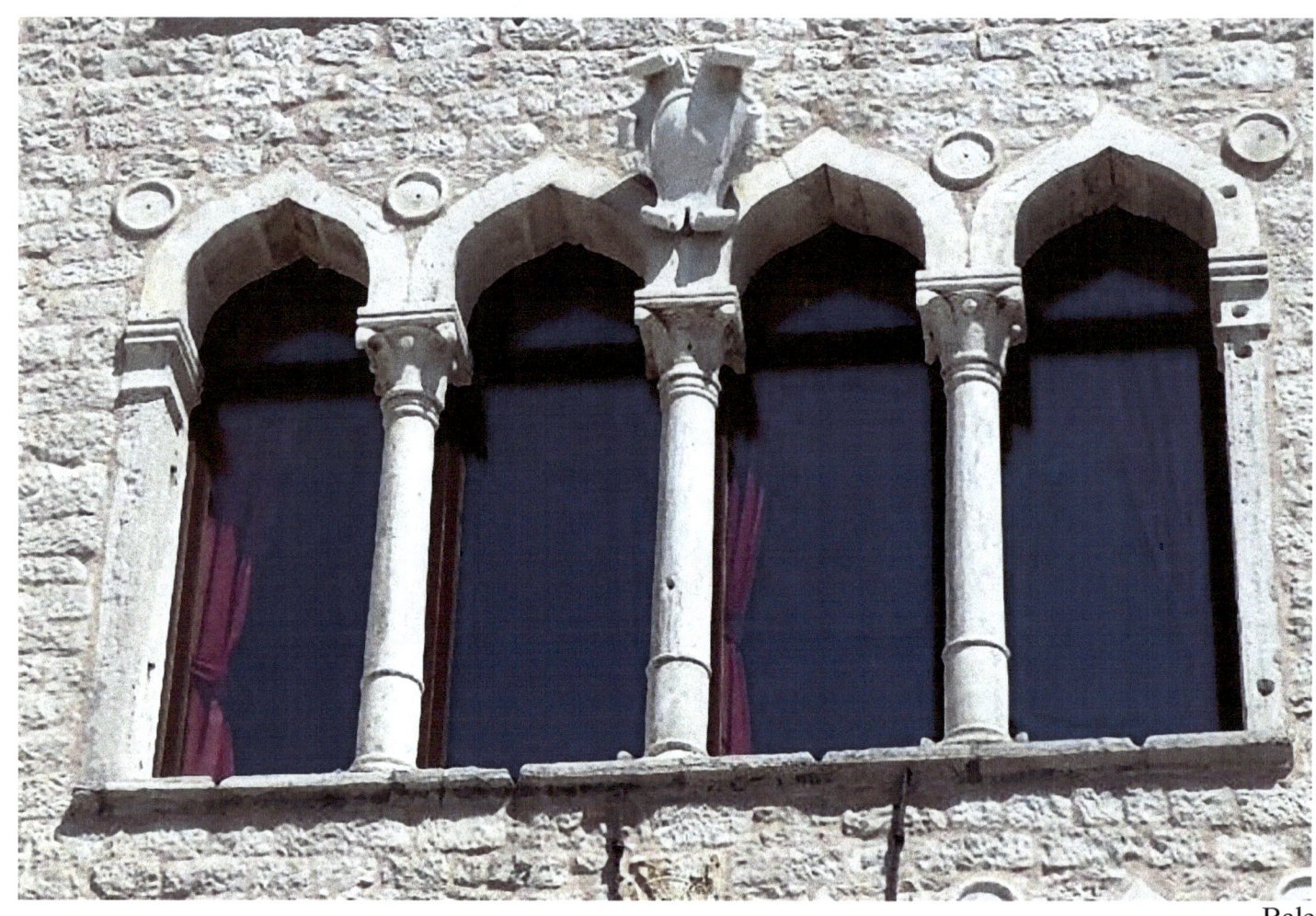

Bale

Pogača, stuffed focaccia. Prepare a flour mixture with a little oil and yeast, and when it is risen divide into two parts, form two rectangles with the rolling pin and let them rest. Place one rectangle on the pan forming a base, sprinkle it with tomatoes, anchovies, garlic, blonde onion, chopped capers and cover everything with the second rectangle of dough. Place in hot oven at 180 ° for 45 minutes.

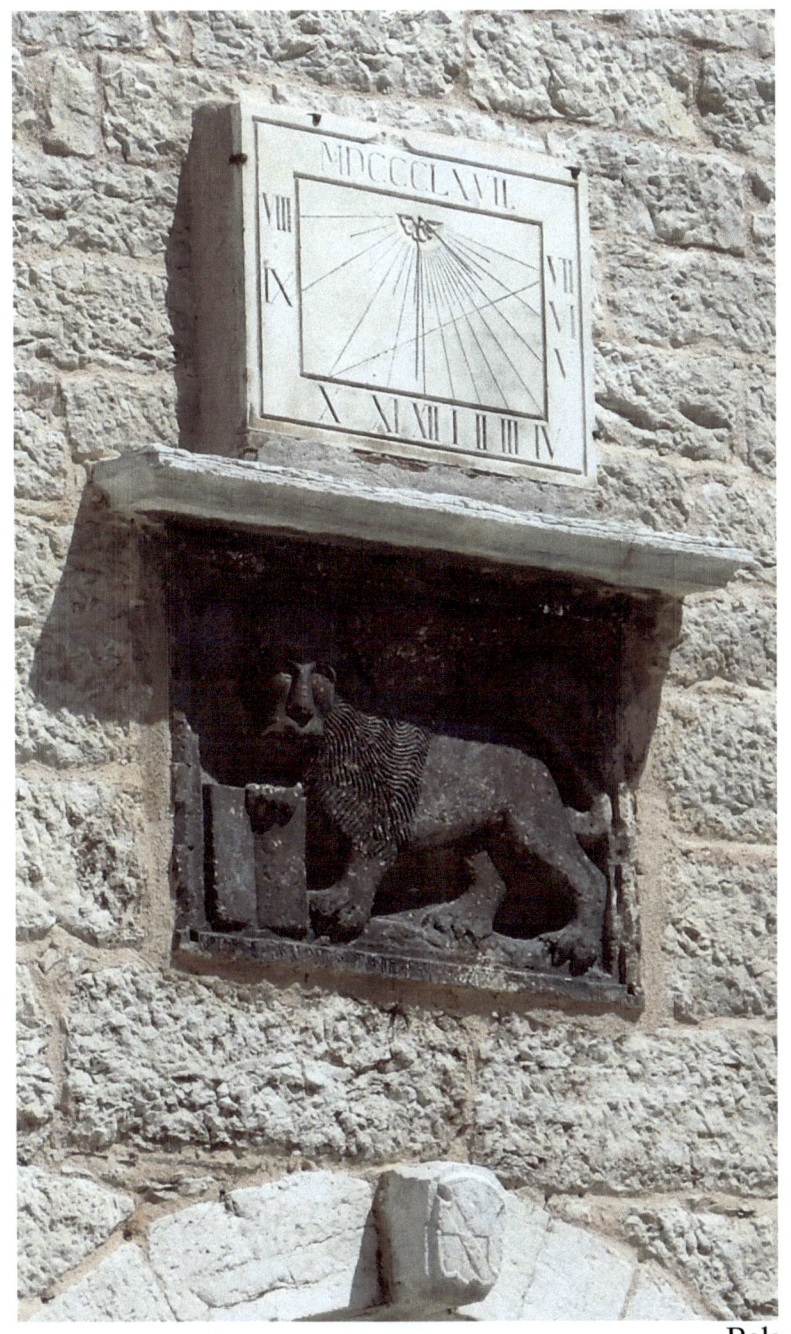

Bale

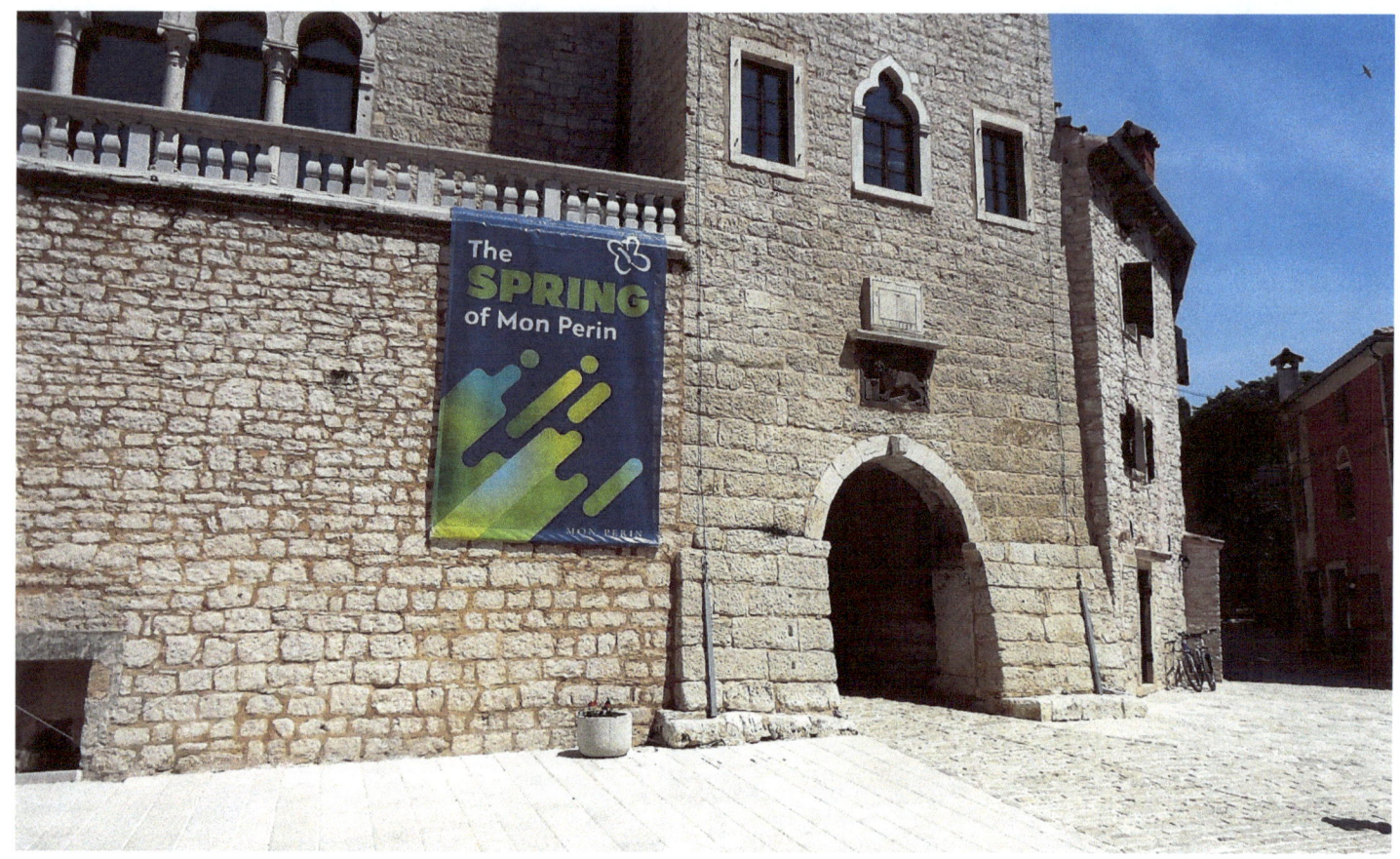

Bale

Štrudla, strudel. A typical autumnal dish where the dough is prepared with flour, sugar, water, oil and salt, and the filling with apples, dried biscuits, pine nuts and butter, with a final addition of icing sugar. For the puff pastry, sift the flour, add the butter to pieces and work it adding lukewarm water until it becomes an smooth and homogeneous dough, which does not stick to the hands. Then form a ball, cover it with a cloth and let it rest for at least 30 minutes…

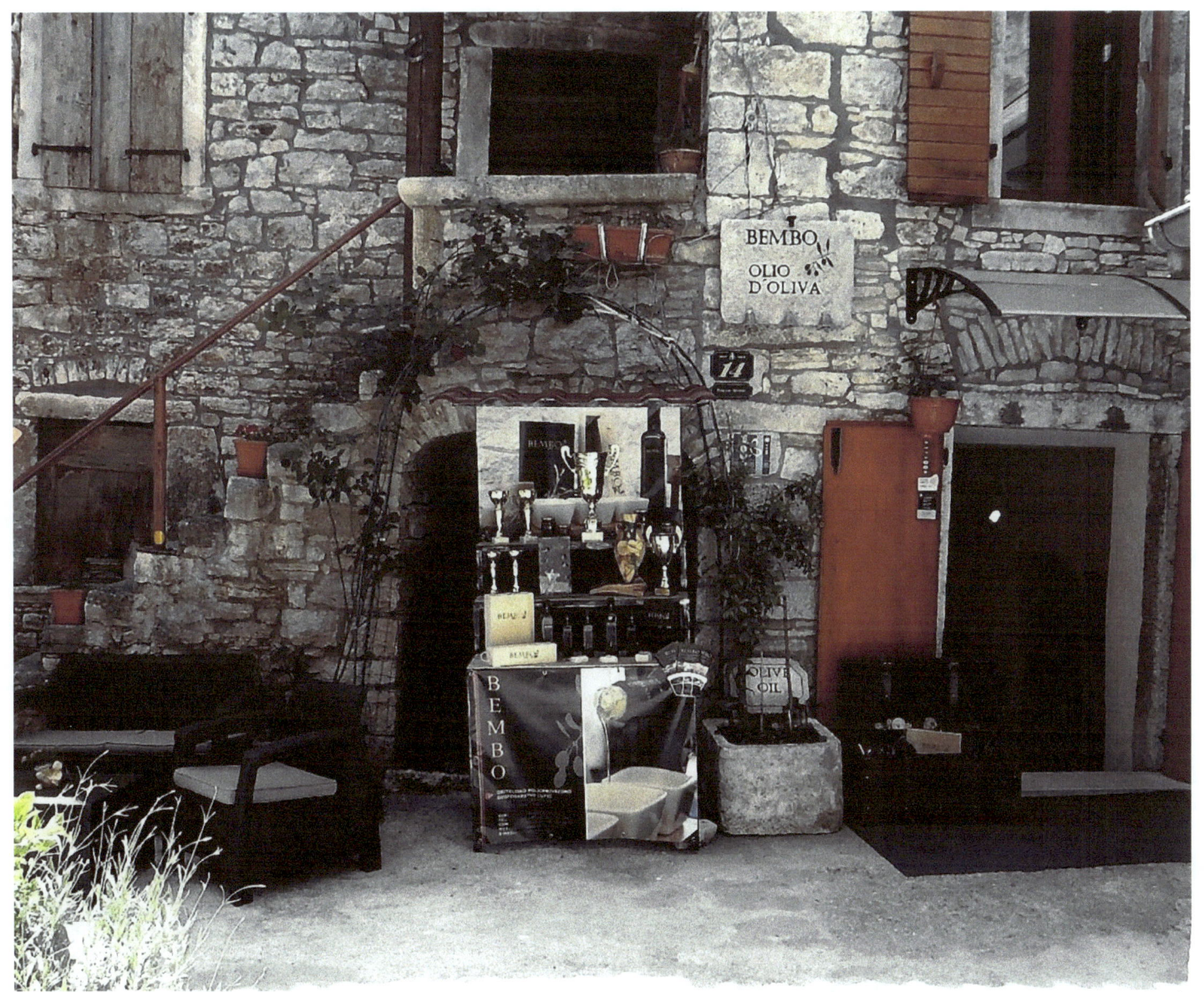

Bale

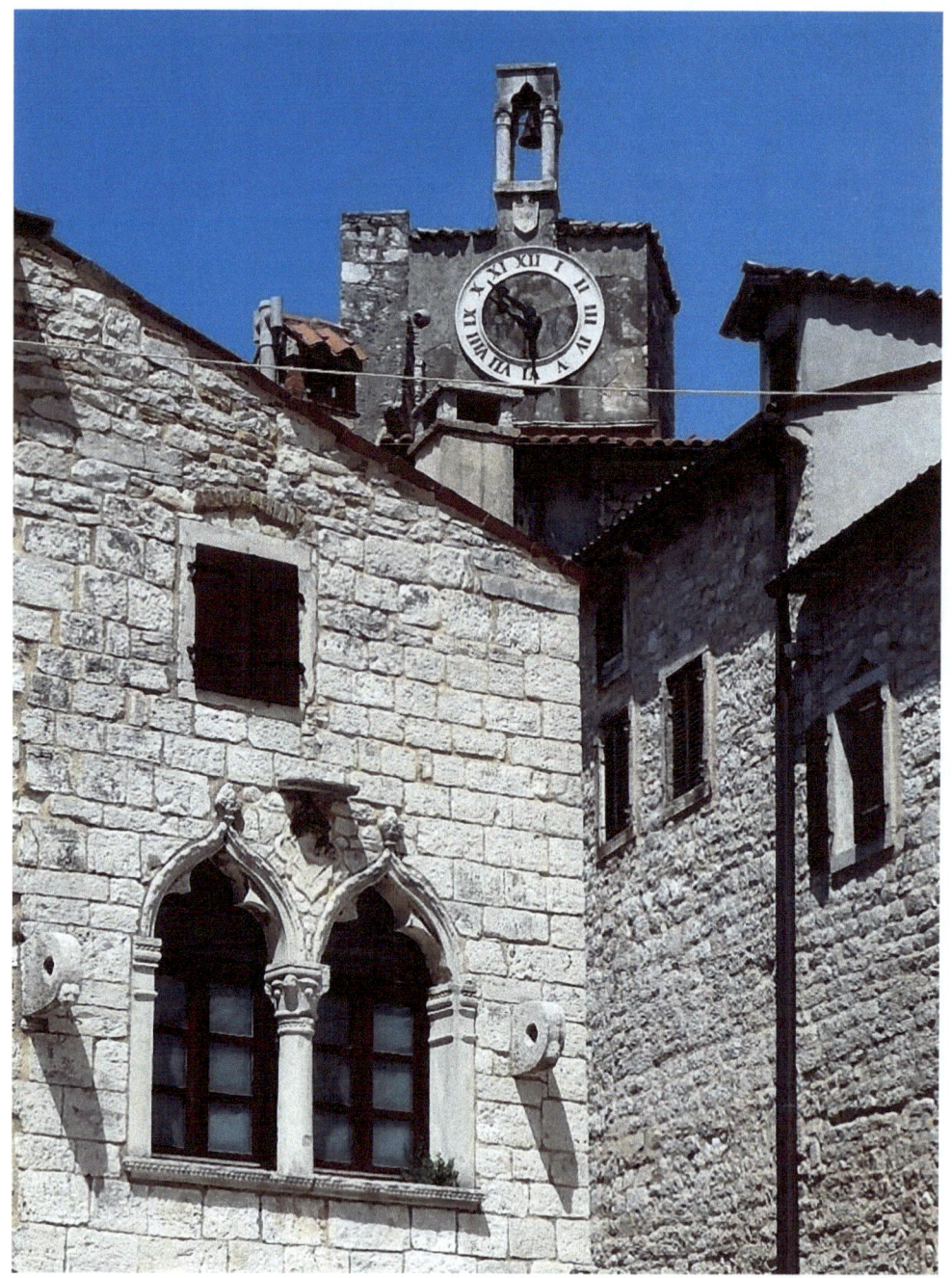

Bale

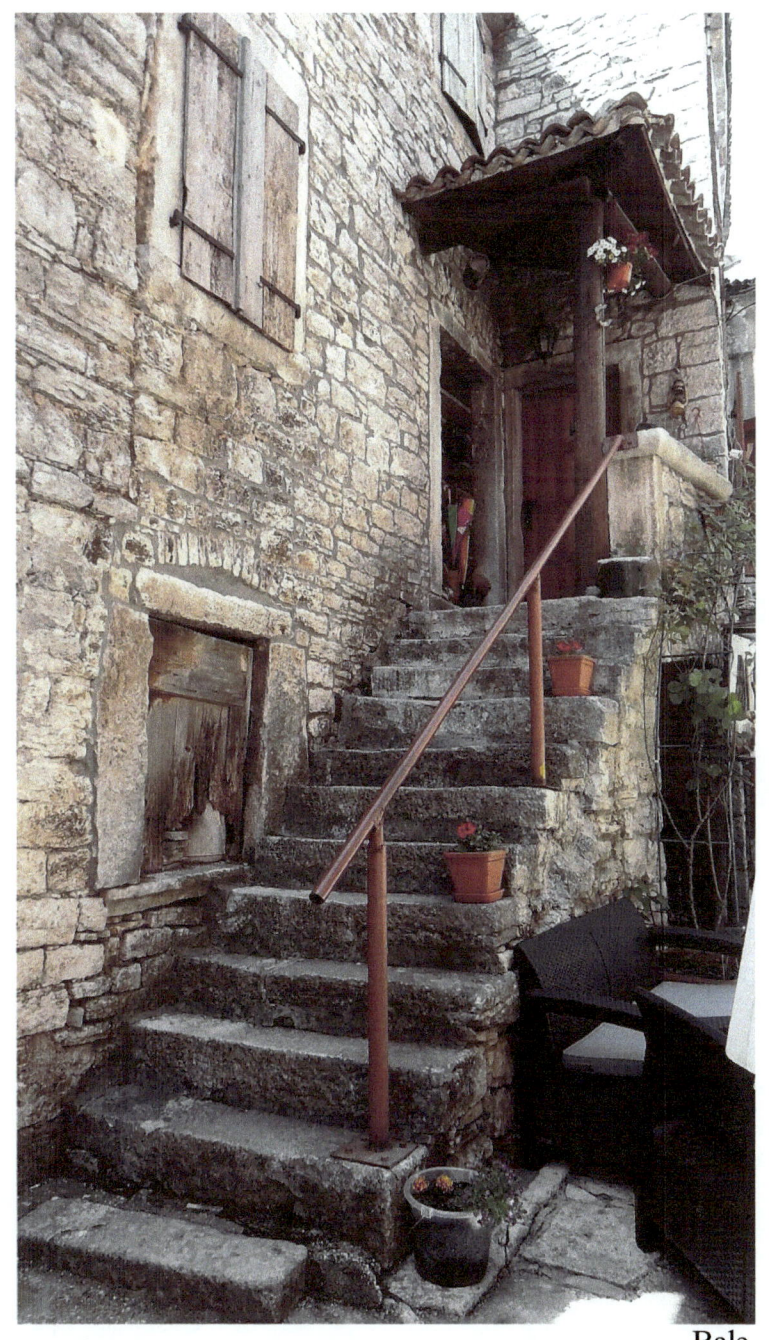

Bale

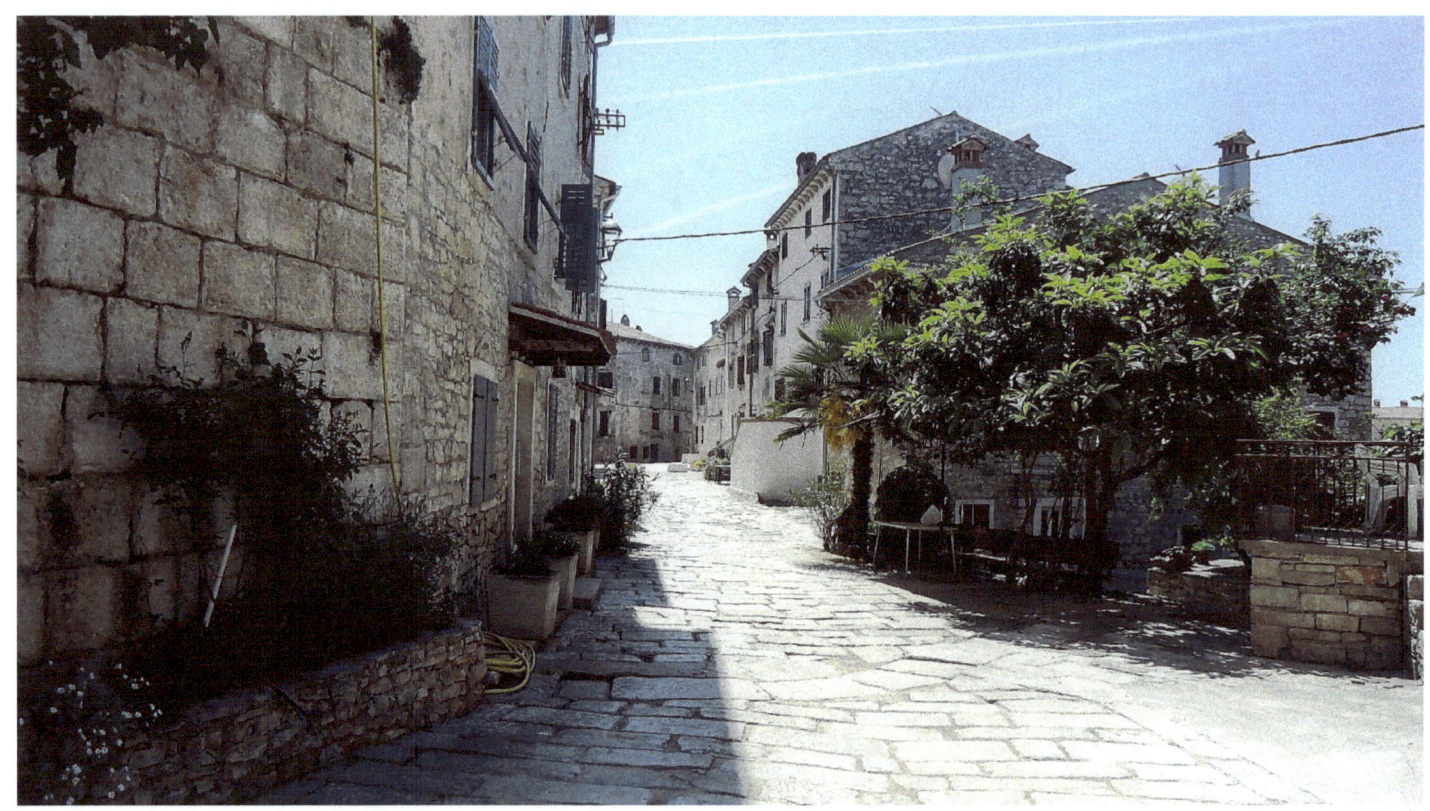

Bale

…For the filling, peel the apples and cut them into thin slices, put the raisins in water for at least 30 minutes, then remove from the water and squeeze them. Crumble the sponge cake, combine the sugar with softened butter and in small pieces. Mix until the compound is homogeneous, add the raisins, the sponge cake, the pine nuts, a pinch of salt and a cinnamon. Combine the apples, always stirring, break the egg and separate the yolk from the white. Spread the dough with the roller until it becomes very thin, spread the filling over the dough, roll it by forming a cylinder and close its two ends by pressing the margins. Place it on a cloth, brush the surface with egg yolk, flour a baking pan and place it on the strudel, overthrow it on the baking pan, arrange it in the desired shape and sprinkle the surface with the egg white. Bake at 180 ° C for 45 minutes. Remove from the oven and allow to cool. Place it on a serving plate and decorate with powdered sugar.

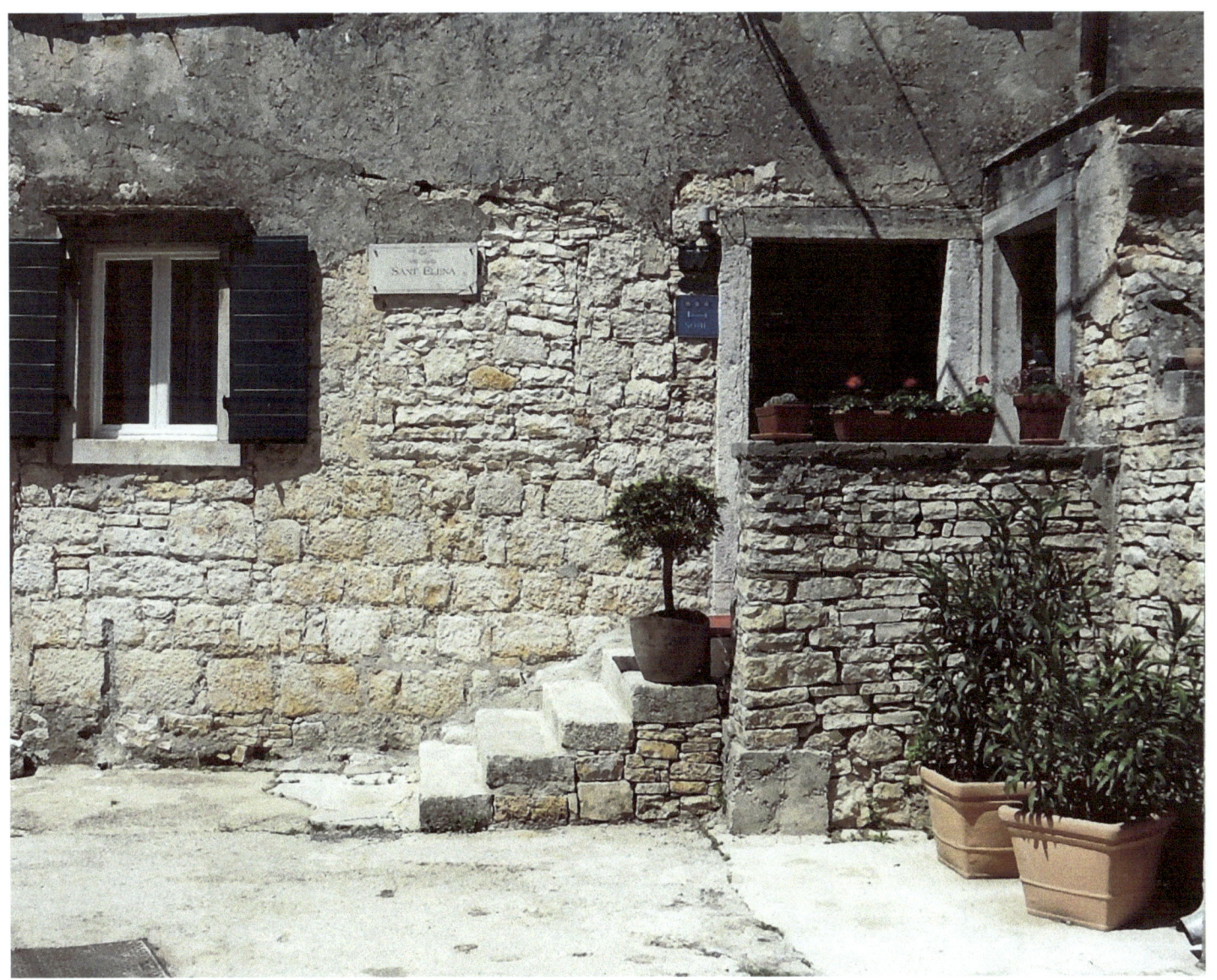

Bale

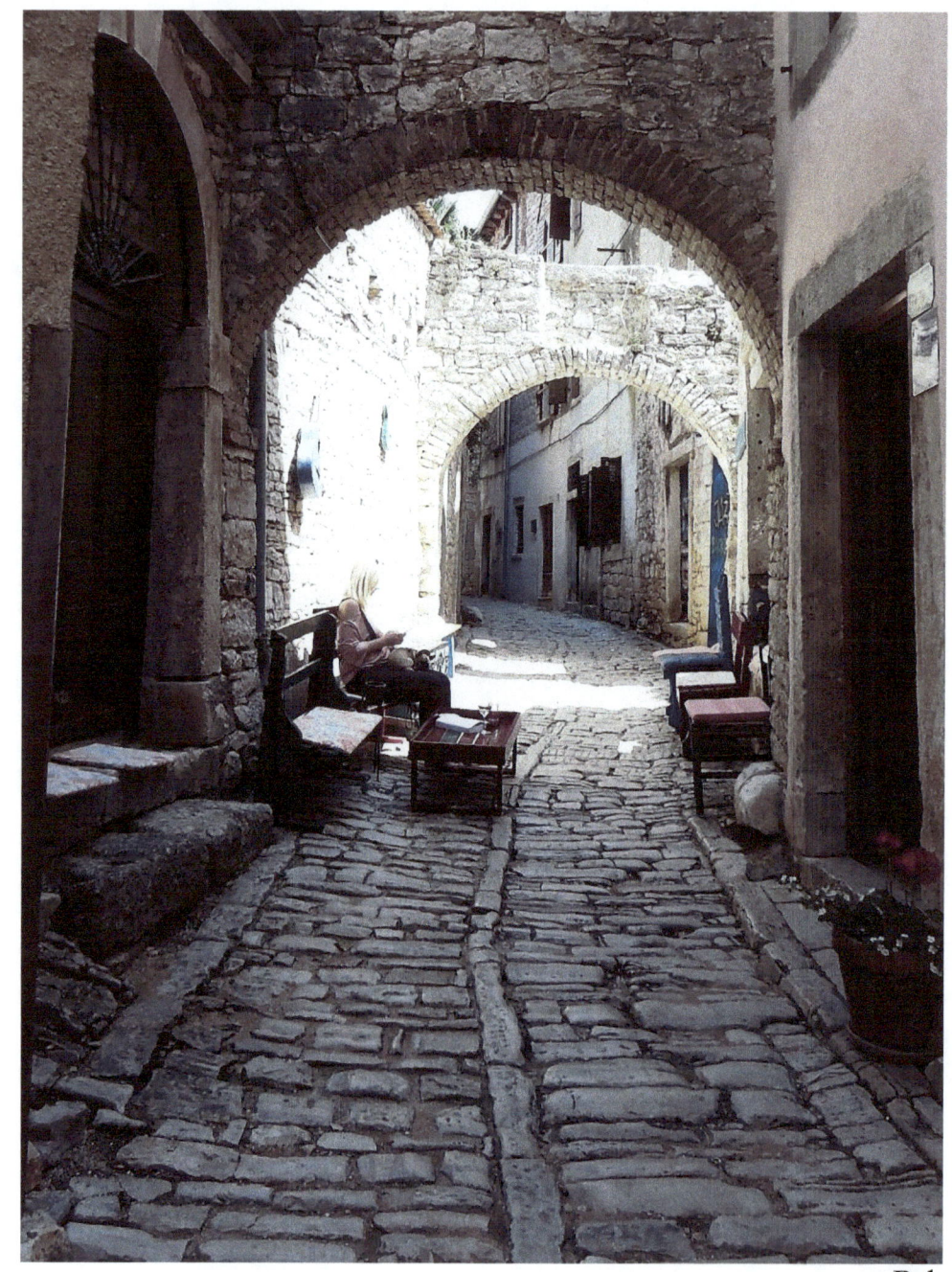

Bale

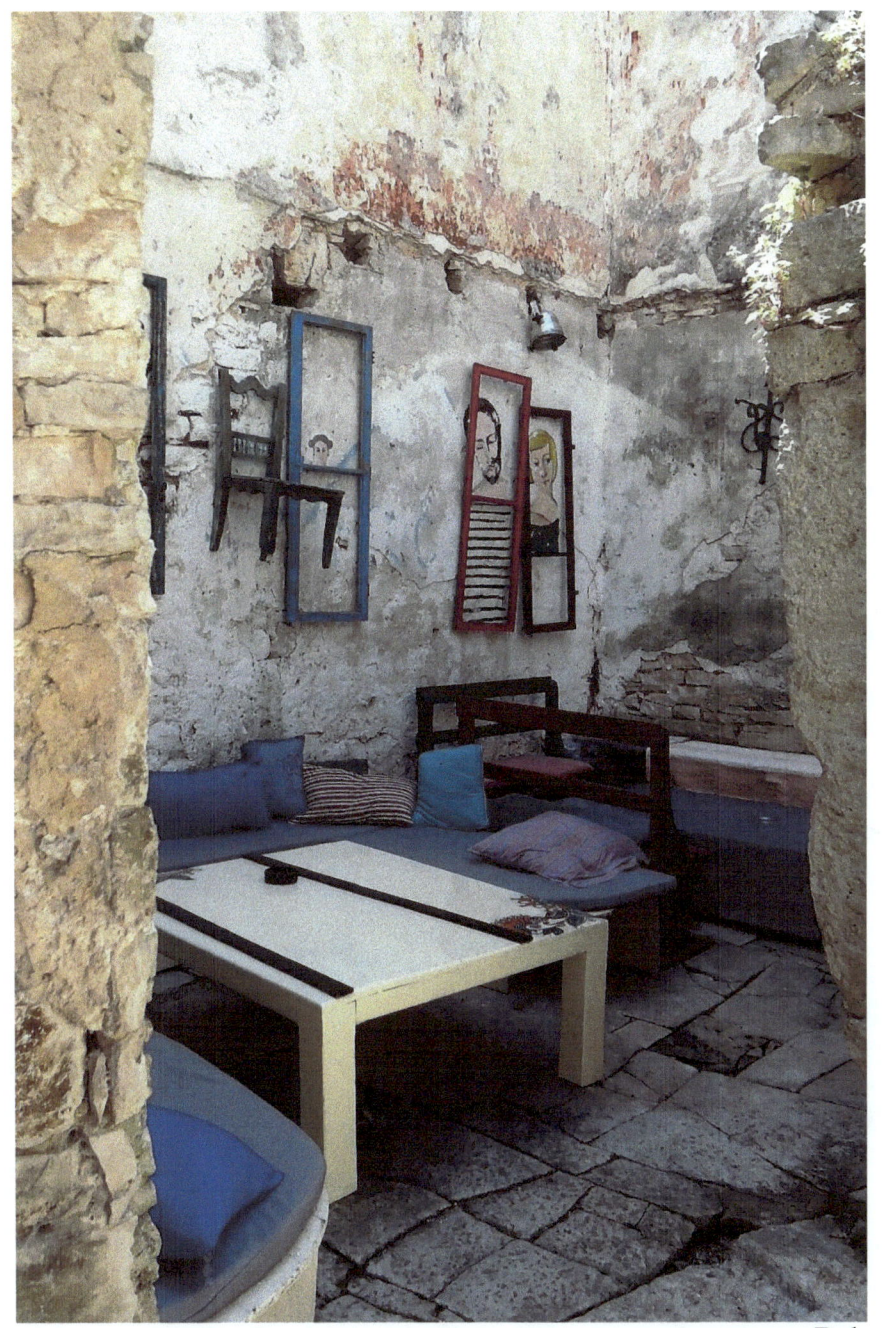

Bale

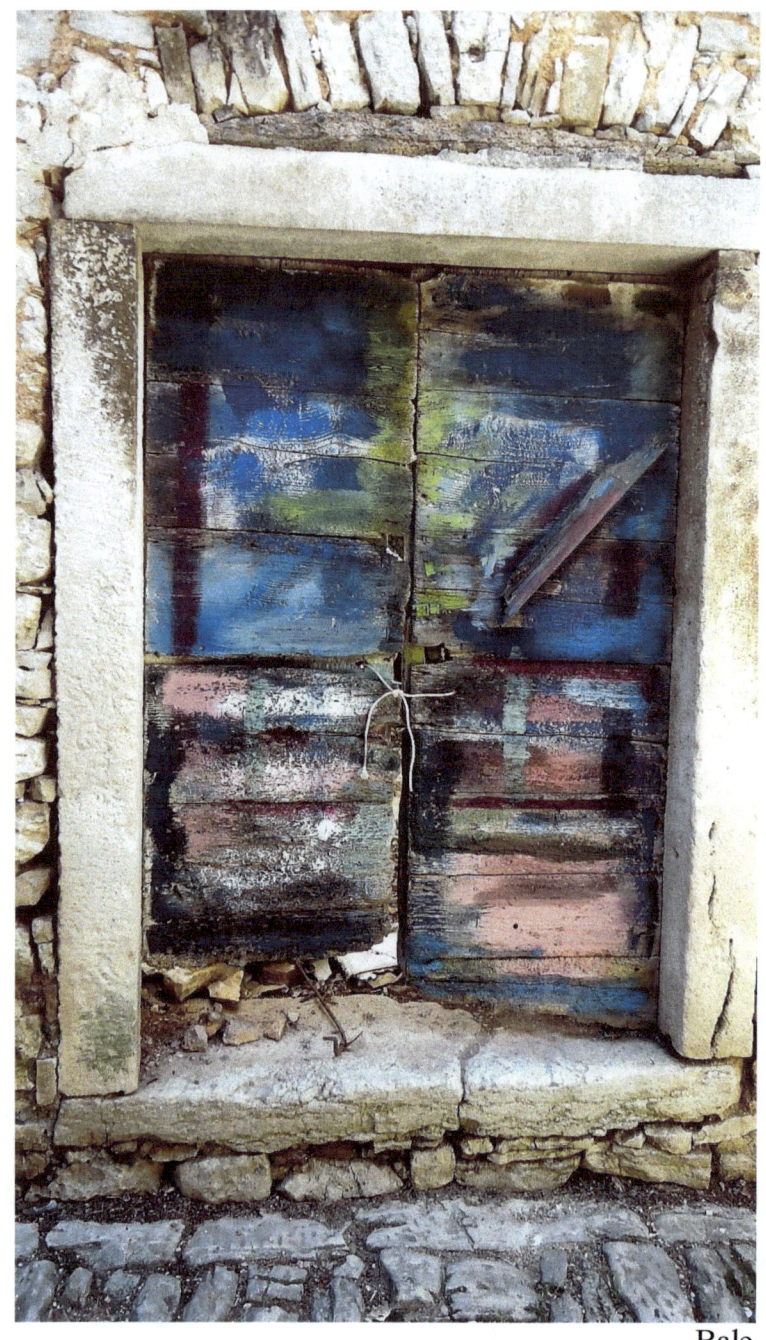

Bale

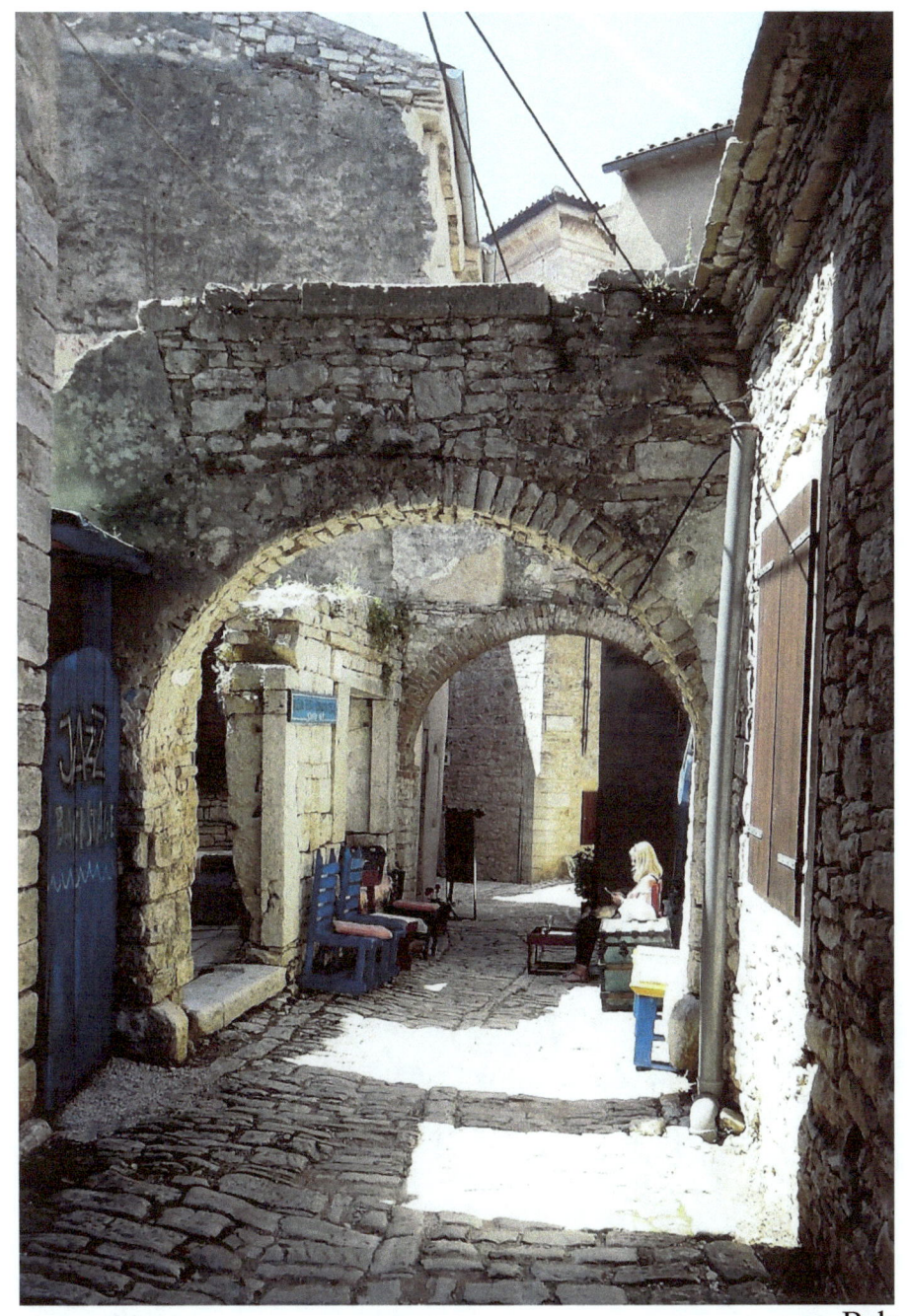

Bale

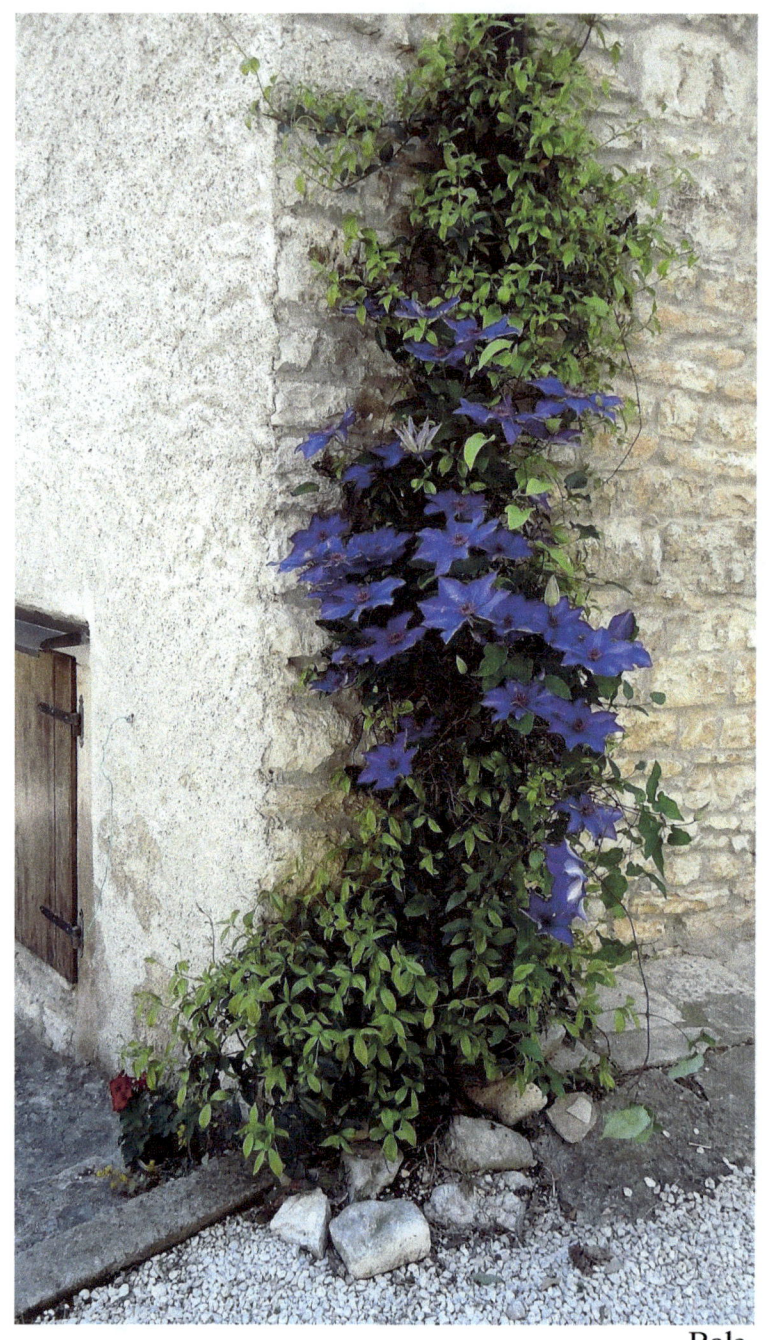

Bale